the
healing
energies
of
colour

how to use this book

This book presents a comprehensive summary of the scientific basis of colour therapy, of the treatments and techniques used, and of how to treat with colour. There are also exercises and practical activities, indicated by a solid bar above the text. By following the instructions you can begin your therapeutic work in colour at home.

The book can be used on its own or in conjunction with a professional training in colour therapy. For a professional qualification you will require a personal tutor (see Resources, p. 124).

For diagnosis and treatment of serious illness, you should always consult a qualified colour practitioner. Under the professional code of practice for colour practitioners, all colour therapy treatments for serious illness should be given under medical supervision. Colour therapy can be used successfully in conjunction with Western medicine.

foreword

The power of colour is a part of the natural energy of the universe. When we learn to see beyond the manifest physical world, we gain an insight into the principles at work in the universe and begin to have a vision of the full beauty and inter-connectedness of everything around us. As part of the spectrum of natural energies emanating from the sun, colour surrounds us. It fills our bodies and interacts with our own energies, and has been used since early times to heal.

Colour healing was part of the ancient wisdom taught and practised in the great temples of Egypt and Greece, in China, India, and Tibet. It was part of the Mayan culture of Central America, and the tribal lore of the North American Indians. These teachings influenced the Greek schools of philosophy, such as those of Pythagoras and Plato, but then all but disappeared in the West in the Dark Ages. The medieval craftsmen who designed the glorious Gothic cathedrals knew of them, but it was not until the nineteenth century that the work of Newton, Goethe and others, revived interest in the properties of light and colour. Now some of the teachings preserved in ancient literatures have been rediscovered and their tenets and techniques incorporated into a modern scientific framework. This book presents some of that knowledge and provides a comprehensive array of therapies that are a valuable adjunct to the practice of natural healing. These range from the simple to the profound; from the everyday use of colour in clothes and cosmetics to the specialist application of coloured shapes, crystals, oils, and light.

Patterns of energy interactions within and around the human body are similar to those that occur around every living entity in nature. Although they are not normally visible to the human eye, they can be seen using the techniques of Kirlian photography, and appear as an enveloping aura, as shown in the illustration of a leaf on the facing page. Illness develops out of imbalances of energies that may have occurred or been created at the emotional or spiritual levels, or that result from changes at a physical level, such as the effects of bacteria and viruses. With this understanding you will see how the techniques of colour therapy described in this book can assist the body to heal itself. They are a powerful tool in treating the whole range of disease, from minor ailments, such as headaches and listlessness, to chronic disorders, where by rebalancing and revitalizing the body's energies, treatment with colour can support and augment other treatments and therapies. Colour therapy is also especially useful in the treatment of stress-related skin disorders, such as eczema and psoriasis, and of depression, including SAD (seasonal affective disorder).

By extending your understanding of the natural colour energies and developing your awareness of their power, This Book will open your eyes and your mind to the miraculous world of colour.

CONTENTS

introduction   *10-13*

CHAPTER ONE

colour in our world   *14-29*

THE IMPORTANCE OF COLOUR   17
HISTORY OF COLOUR   21
COLOUR IN MAKE-UP AND CLOTHES   23
COLOUR IN THE HOME AND AT WORK   25
DECORATION SUMMARY CHART   29

CHAPTER TWO

the science of colour   *30-41*

HISTORY OF COLOUR SCIENCE   33
THE EXTENDED SPECTRUM   37
LIGHT AND PIGMENT   39
COMPLEMENTARY COLOURS   41

CHAPTER THREE

feeling the effects of colour   *42-57*

INTUITIVE KNOWLEDGE OF COLOUR   45
COLOUR AND FORM   47
COLOUR AND THE SENSES   49
COLOUR MEDITATION   53
COLOUR AND MOVEMENT   57

CHAPTER FOUR

colour energies in the body   *58-77*

ENERGY INPUT AND OUTPUT   61
THE HUMAN AURA   63
CHAKRAS   65

DETECTING COLOUR ENERGIES   67
COLOUR IN THE SPINE   69
DOWSING THE SPINE   71
THE COLOURS OF HEALTH   73
VARIATIONS IN THE AURA   77

CHAPTER FIVE

feeling off colour   78-97

ILLNESS AND ITS DIAGNOSIS   81
THE CHALLENGE OF ILLNESS   83
WORKING WITH A COUNSELLOR   85
ILLNESS AND THE AURA   89
DIAGNOSING COLOUR CHANGES   91
COLOUR REFLECTION READING   95
THE LÜSCHER TEST   97

CHAPTER SIX

healing with colour   98-123

TREATMENT TECHNIQUES   101
COLOUR CONSCIOUSNESS EXERCISE   103
WORKING WITH COLOURED PIGMENT   105
HEALING WITH LIGHT   107
COLOUR THERAPY INSTRUMENTS   109
THE TREATMENT COLOURS   111
COLOUR HEALING ACCESSORIES   117
CASE STUDIES   121

resources   124

index   125-127

introduction

Colour is an experience. It is one that we, on this planet, are uniquely privileged to enjoy.

The spectrum of electromagnetic energies that emanate from the sun and irradiate the Earth includes the range that we "see" as light. The varying wavelengths of this energy are reflected back to our eyes from the objects they strike and interpreted by our brains as the various hues of the colour spectrum, so that when we view the world in terms of colour, in fact, the colour is in our minds, not in the landscape. As John Stewart Collis says in *The Vision of Glory:*

> *"We see the yellow daffodil growing up out of the ground, and it seems clear that its colour, the most emphatic thing about it, grows up with it, belongs to it. Yet no; that yellow on the daffodil, that red on the rose was eight minutes ago in the sun.*

This manifestation of colour results from a very fine balance of factors: the receptive abilities of our eyes and brain, and the combination of gases, moisture, and dust particles in the Earth's atmosphere that filter, reflect, and refract the rays of light energy. Without this atmosphere there would be no life on Earth and little colour. Too many particles in the atmosphere, either from

natural causes or industrial pollution, can create a blanket that some of the light rays cannot penetrate. When the light level is reduced in this way, or when it declines gradually at dusk, the colour experience fades and we are left in a world of monotones.

None of us see colour in quite the same way, or to the same intensity. We tend to think of it as a purely physical phenomenon experienced by our sense of sight alone, but as a form of energy, colour is active at all levels of our being – mental, emotional, physical, and spiritual. Hence its effects are not restricted only to the sighted. Those with impaired vision are equally receptive to these energies, and in many cases are more so because of their enhanced sensitivity to non-visual stimuli.

As you work through this book, you will discover that each colour has its individual characteristics and effects. Some of these you may use intuitively in your dress and make-up to reveal or disguise your true feelings and intentions; some will already be familiar to you as everyday cliches used to express emotions and feelings: "red with anger", "green with envy". Extremes of emotions are often the outward display of imbalances or blockages in the flow of colour energies into and out of the body. Analysis of these imbalances can reveal ailments before they manifest in the physical body, and colour therapy treatments, such as controlled exposure to coloured light, can adjust and correct the energy flow.

The later chapters of this book describe techniques of colour diagnosis such as perceiving and interpreting the coloured aura that surrounds all living things, and using a pendulum to dowse the colour energies in the vertebrae of the spine. There are charts to aid the analysis and diagnosis of illness, and the choice of suitable treatments. Some of these are straightforward enough for you to work at on your own: a change of colour scheme in your home or workplace may be all that is needed. In some cases more advanced techniques may be called for, such as the use of crystals or coloured light. These will require the guidance of a trained practitioner.

The exercises in this book, in particular the breathing, visualization, and meditation exercises, will enable you to raise your colour perception and fine-tune your senses to open yourself up to the healing colour energies. You will enjoy the benefits of this active approach to colour at all levels of your being – physical, mental, emotional and, most importantly, spiritual.

Without life there is little colour; without colour there is no life.

CHAPTER ONE

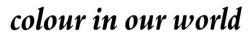

colour in our world

The importance of colour

We are bathed in colour all our lives, even from the moment of conception: light penetrates translucent skin and muscle to envelop the developing fetus in a reddish-golden glow. Born into a world of colours, we grow surrounded by colour in the environment and in our homes; we dress in colourful clothes, eat colourful foods, and make choices that are informed by colour every day. Rarely if at all do we have a colourless experience: a white space without form, or complete darkness. Instead, through the changing contrast of dark and light we perceive the colours in our human world and our surroundings.

Colour dominates our senses. We learn at an early age to interpret our environment as much by colour as by shapes or sounds. Our response to colour is so basic that, until the age of about five, six, or even later, children who are asked to sort coloured shapes automatically divide them according to their colour, rather than their shape. Boys and girls develop in slightly different ways: whereas girls maintain their level of response to colour, boys start to respond more to shape at an earlier age.

Throughout life we continue to use colour as a cue for interpreting what we see: grey hair tells us of middle age; grey landscapes speak of cities; a red apple tells of its ripeness; red traffic lights bring us to a halt. Colour coding guides our travels, our administration, and such practical details as electric wiring. Colour gives us information about much of our environment; it even helps us to locate ourselves geographically, by the hue of the local stone, for example, or the tones of the colours in a landscape.

Colour messages

At another level, we make statements about our mood with the colours we wear, and we can read how our friends feel, too, through their colour statements. The colours we see around us can noticeably affect our states of mind and our feelings – the colour in a red room produces very different sensations from those in a room painted blue. Colour schemes alter the amount and the type of light that our eyes, our skin, and even the underlying tissues and organs receive. And colour is strongly linked with emotions. By describing

Darkness and light

The Bible says, "In the beginning God created the heaven and the earth.

And the earth was without form, and void; and darkness was upon the face of the deep. And the spirit of God moved upon the face of the waters.

And God said, Let there be light: and there was light."

Genesis 1:1

The energy of light came out of darkness: darkness pervaded the world before light appeared. We need both light and darkness in our lives, just as seeds need both darkness and light to germinate.

God sleeps in the stone
God dreams in the plant
God moves in the animal
God awakes in man

*Translated from Ancient
Chinese wisdom*

people as "green with envy", "purple with rage", "yellow
with cowardice", or "seeing red", we are using common
colour associations that may have more truth than we realize.

Such associations are only part of our lifelong relationship
with colour: we live by the rhythm of colour changes that
denote the passage of time and the cycle of seasons. As day
passes, the daylight colours change and are infinitely mobile
in their hues. The deep blue of the sky before dawn gives
way to the paler blue light that permeates mornings; this is
followed by the more yellow hue of the afternoon and then
the red light of the evening. These shifts can be so gradual
that they are hardly noticeable, but nonetheless they colour
our perception of the passing day (see right). The seasons,
too, highlight very different colours, with the fresh greens
of spring darkening as the summer progresses, and providing

Colour and photography
*You can experiment with your camera
to see how colours change during the
course of a clear day. Find a place
where you can take pictures of green
grass, blue sky, and some red or
orange objects, such as flowers, in the
early morning, mid-morning, at mid-
day, in the mid-afternoon, and in the
early evening.*

a blaze of orange, yellow, and gold only a few months later. Winter introduces a stark note, with few vivid colours, and sometimes a smattering of snow that obliterates the remaining green, reducing the outlook to a simple contrast between darkness and light. Many of us live in houses that offer light at any time of the day and night, and heat or coolness throughout the year, and so to some extent we lose contact with the natural rhythms of the daily and yearly cycles.

Light as visible energy

Our eyes translate the energy of light into signals – nervous impulses – that the brain interprets as "seeing". This visible light is part of a wider spectrum of energy that surrounds us (see p. 34), and most of this comes from the sun. Visible light is made up of the colours that we know as the rainbow. Our eyes are sensitive to the whole range of its hues, but the rest of the spectrum is invisible to us. Although these energies, such as infrared and ultraviolet, are outside our conscious colour vision, we are nonetheless sensitive to them to some extent (see left).

Light and its constituent colours have a strong effect on both mind and body. At physical, mental, and emotional levels we respond to colours whether we realize it or not.

Physical responses to colour

As a general rule, the red end of the spectrum tends to make the body tense, while the blue end of the spectrum tends to relax it. Exposure to red increases the blood pressure, while blue relaxes the body and lowers blood pressure (see p. 20).

Mental responses to colour

Colour affects our perceptions. A red room seems smaller than a blue one, for example.

Emotional responses to colour

Colour affects the way we feel about what we see. This is connected to the physical responses and psychological associations developed from infancy onward. But in general, red excites us, while blue makes us feel more calm.

Colour and physiology

Colour not only fills our outside world; it penetrates deep into our bodies. Its continual influence means that the effects of light on the body are second only to the effects of food.

Responding to the invisible

In addition to visible light the sun emits high-energy cosmic rays, gamma rays, X-rays, and ultraviolet, which have a subtle impact on us all the time. The Earth's atmosphere, in particular the ozone layer, protects us from much of their harmful effects. Little is documented about the way in which this background radiation affects us.

The stained-glass window from Chartres Cathedral in France (right), transforms daylight into colours rich in spiritual overtones. The craft of creating stained glass, which reached its height in Europe during the 12th and 13th centuries, relies heavily on the ability of metallic oxides to "hold" the light and generate an atmosphere suitable for meditation and prayer.

Experiments on plants, which need light in order to make carbohydrates, show that exposing them only to red or green light, for example, radically alters the quality of their growth. When mustard and cress seeds were exposed to only red light, the developing plants were stunted with small foliage, and had a bitter taste. Exposure to only green light produced weak plants. In contrast, under blue light the seeds produced beautiful, well developed plants, which grew quite slowly, and had a very sweet flavour.

Of all the colours, red and blue light have the most marked effect on the physiology of the human body. Red light increases muscular activity, blood pressure, respiration, and heart rate. Blue has the opposite effect, relaxing the body, and can help insomnia sufferers (see also p. 101).

The pathways of light

Light energy received by the eye sets up nervous impulses on the retina, which travel as coded messages along the optic nerve to the visual cortex at the back of the brain. En route, some of these excitations trigger a specific part of the brain's hypothalamus, which acts as the body's biological clock by regulating sleeping, feeding, and other functions such as temperature and water balance.

The hypothalamus influences both the pituitary and pineal glands in the brain. These glands also respond to messages from all the body cells about the quantity and colour quality of light shining on the body.

The pituitary and pineal glands conduct the functions of the body by producing hormones that stimulate other glands, such as the adrenals and reproductive organs, and affect the metabolism of the body.

The effect of colour on our bodies does not depend on our eyesight alone. The superficial layers of skin and flesh – and even the skull – are particularly sensitive to ultraviolet light. Exposure to blue light over the whole body has long been a cure for children with jaundice, and ultraviolet light causes the skin to produce melanin (which gives us a tan) and vitamin D (which is crucial for the body's metabolism of calcium). In Russia, schoolchildren exposed to a supplement of invisible ultraviolet light apparently grew faster, had fewer colds, and produced better work. Experiments have shown that visually impaired people are affected by colour in the same way as the sighted. Some are sensitive enough to identify a colour with great accuracy by feeling the density of the air that surrounds it. The air over a red surface, for example, feels more dense than the air next to blue.

Incoming information from the visible and invisible parts of the spectrum is integrated and taken to every cell in the body (see left). This mechanism helps to orchestrate and harmonize our inner selves with the universe outside.

Too much or too little light can upset general health and wellbeing. People who are exposed to insufficient light, either because they spend too much time indoors in artificial light, which does not provide the full spectrum found in natural daylight energy (see Chapter Two), or because they live in latitudes where the sun is absent for long periods during the winter, are known to be prone to winter-time depression (see p. 37). By contrast, excessive exposure to light has been shown to speed development, and even have an ageing effect. For example, girls who live in towns and cities where the night is kept artificially light by high levels of street lighting, begin menstruation earlier than girls from more rural areas, who experience a normal day/night rhythm of light and darkness.

History of Colour

Egypt
The ancient Egyptians listed on a papyrus from 1550BC a number of coloured cures, including red lead, black lizards, and verdigris, a green copper salt which, when mixed with beetle wax, was used to treat cataracts. The Egyptians are said to have built temples where colour healing took place. Sunlight shone through coloured gems, such as rubies and sapphires, on to people seeking healing. They also used pulverized gemstones as remedies for sickness – yellow beryls, for example, as a cure for jaundice.

China
The Chinese have always diagnosed illness by reading the "colour" of pulses, complexion, and the appearance of the body's tissues and organs. A red pulse indicates numbness of the heart, whereas a yellow pulse means the stomach is healthy. The *Nei Ching,* a medical text compiled almost 2000 years ago, records colour diagnoses. "When the viscera are green like kingfishers' wings they are filled with life." On the other hand, "When their colour is green like grass they are without life."

Europe
Colour was also vital to the doctrine of the Four Humours. This system of medical thought may have originated in Egypt and was common throughout Europe from the days of the ancient Greeks and Romans to the Renaissance. Each humour was assigned its own colour – red blood, black bile, yellow bile, and white phlegm. Any imbalance in the humours was manifested in the colour of the skin complexion, tongue, urine, and faeces.

Correcting imbalances
Colour practitioners can correct imbalances of energy inside the body using a variety of techniques that have been tried and tested over the last hundred years or more. The techniques include the use of full-spectrum lamps, coloured crystals, silks, and shapes; wearing coloured clothes, drinking solarized water, eating colourful foods, and the application of coloured oils during massage (see Chapter Six). In addition, the techniques of colour visualization, colour breathing, and the use of movement enhance the effects of colour (see Chapter Three). A colour practitioner may receive training in any or all of these techniques. The use of full-spectrum lamps in healing is probably the most powerful of the techniques available to the colour practitioner.

Colour in make-up and clothes

For most of us, our awareness of colour begins and ends with our clothes (and, for some of us, our make-up), and the colours of the rooms that surround us at home, at work, or in places we visit.

Our choice of clothes reflects the way we feel; the colours can also contribute to a healing process (see p. 105). Cosmetic psychologists claim that a woman can feel better about herself by adding particular colours to her face, and so begin a cycle of wellbeing. Real confidence, of course, springs from within and a naturally glowing face is the result of good health and diet, as well as happiness and wellbeing – the inner harmony on which colour practitioners work.

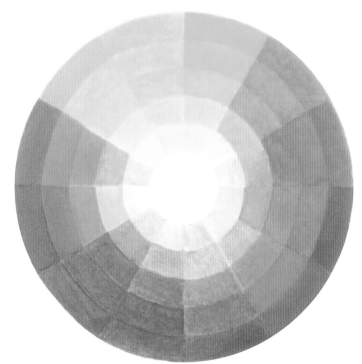

The Itten colour wheel

Johannes Itten's work at the Bauhaus School led him to develop a graphic device that would enable artists to visualize the result of mixing colours (left).

Primary pigment colours are mixed to produce secondaries. For example, the primaries yellow and red make orange, a secondary colour. Mixing orange and yellow produces orangey-yellow, a tertiary colour. Itten's wheel demonstrated how adding black and white affected each colour; the importance of this came from Itten's observations that colours appeared harmonious if, together, they yielded a neutral shade of grey.

Cosmetic colours can appear to alter the dimensions of your face by changing the colour of your hair, skin, lips, and eye make-up. This may make you feel better about yourself but there is no substitute for the natural face (right), which glows with the spirit of inner wellbeing.

Colour therapy works on this inner harmony. While the superficial applications of coloured fabrics and oils enhance the work of the practitioner, they cannot be as effective as a complete colour treatment using full-spectrum coloured lights.

The origin of cosmetic advice

In an attempt to represent the relationships between colours, and to indicate how one colour affects the appearance of another, Johannes Itten, a lecturer at the Bauhaus School in Germany in the 1920s, developed his colour wheel. Itten expressed colours not only in terms of hue, but in their "cold" or "warm" appearance. Yellow, yellow-orange, orange, red, and red-violet are warm, while yellow-green, green, blue, blue-violet, and violet are cold. The intermediate hues may appear to be more or less warm or cold, depending on their adjacent colours.

Itten was fascinated by designs, and the connections between colour, form, and music. He also noted that his students' colour choices complemented the colours of their skin, hair, and eyes. His observations gave rise to skin colour analysis tests, which formed the basis for a most successful cosmetic consultancy service.

Colour in the home and at work

For thousands of years the number of pigments available for colouring objects was limited. Artists, dyers, glaziers, and other crafts people used pigments such as woad, madder, cochineal, and Tyrian purple, derived from natural sources. The advent of artificial dyes in the latter half of the 19th century led to an explosion of colour that continues to this day. Using modern techniques, small adjustments in the amount of black or white pigment added to the basic colours of the spectrum can create a myriad different tints or shades.

With the wealth of colours now available, information on the particular effects of different colours is now in demand. Colour practitioners can advise on colour use in the home, in hospitals and schools, and in offices and factories.

Colour at school

For a young child of 6 to 7 years, the colour rose pink enhances the child's emotional as well as active involvement in the class. In the Waldorf school in Göttingen, Germany (below), the colour scheme for each year's classroom is subtly different, moving toward yellow for 12 year olds. This reflects their increasing mental activity. For the following year, a gentle green fills the classroom, allowing the teenagers to balance their thoughts and make careful judgements.

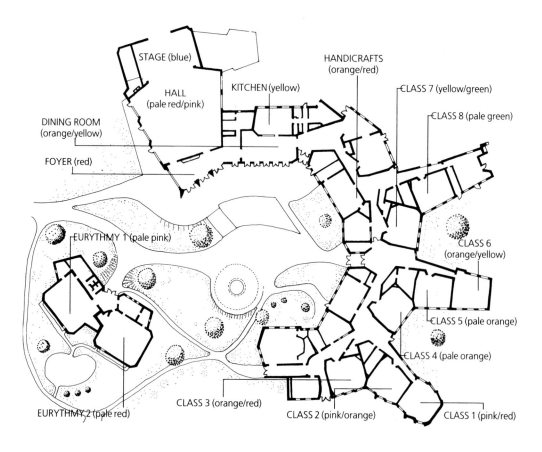

STAGE (blue)

HANDICRAFTS (orange/red)

KITCHEN (yellow)

CLASS 7 (yellow/green)

HALL (pale red/pink)

CLASS 8 (pale green)

DINING ROOM (orange/yellow)

FOYER (red)

EURYTHMY 1 (pale pink)

CLASS 6 (orange/yellow)

CLASS 5 (pale orange)

CLASS 4 (pale orange)

CLASS 3 (orange/red)

CLASS 2 (pink/orange)

CLASS 1 (pink/red)

EURYTHMY 2 (pale red)

Each room in a home can be coloured for a specific purpose. Take your cue from the warm and cool colours (see the Itten colour wheel, p. 22). Use warm colours to stimulate activity in a room; use cool colours to produce a calming effect. Turquoise, for example, is a good colour for a kitchen. It gives a fresh appearance and promotes calm activity. Use bright colours to promote alertness and high-light the parts of the kitchen that are potentially hazardous. Bedrooms need relaxing blues or greens, whereas the colour of a study can tend toward more stimulating shades such as reds or browns, depending on the mood that the work requires. Greens and peachy-orange colours create a peaceful place to digest food and enjoy the company of friends (see the summary chart on pages 28-9).

Rudolf Steiner (1861-1925) studied the effects of colour on individuals and developed a theory from which he pro-duced colour schemes for school rooms. His first school opened in Stuttgart in 1919. Steiner, known for his philo-sophical lectures and his work in education, considered that the most important aspect of a child's learning came directly from the developing spirituality. The scheme of colours that Steiner recommended for each age group is intended to reflect the child's stage of development (see facing page).

Hospital colour schemes can help the healing process. Specially chosen colours in hospitals for the mentally ill have had dramatic effects. The following key words offer a useful basic guidance. They apply to all colour schemes (see pp. 28-9), but have particular relevance for the healing needs of hospitals. Use red to increase energy; orange for joy; yellow for detachment; green to create balance; turquoise for immunity; blue for calmness; violet for dignity, and magenta to help bring about change.

Using these guidelines, blue may well predominate in a hospital for disturbed patients. Use violet at the patients' entrance to give a sense of dignity; orange at the staff entrance to begin the day in a cheerful way. Individual bedrooms can reflect a patient's needs: a lethargic patient, for example, would benefit from a rose-coloured room; use turquoise for those of a nervous disposition, and blue for a restless patient.

The colour of packaging

Psychologist Dr Max Lüscher (see p. 97) put forward the idea that the colour of a product's packaging in some way corresponds to the need that the product fulfils. Products packaged in dark blue, for example, offer security, while someone who chooses a product because of its yellowish-red packaging is revealing a desire to achieve and win.

In offices, factories, and other workplaces the management of colour is used to improve the working environment in order to increase productivity and efficiency. More companies and organizations are making colour an integral part of a building's structure.

Green helps staff tolerate a noisy environment, blue is good for cooling down a hot workplace, and occasional architectural features painted red keep people moving. However, too much of a colour can have a different effect from the one intended – excess red brings out aggression, for example, while too much green makes staff over-relaxed. Safety features, likewise, are based on the effects of exposure to particular colours. Firefighting equipment, for example, is coloured red, as are signs indicating "stop", "don't", or "danger". Green is commonly used to denote an "escape route" or emergency exit.

Commercial products

Companies study and make use of our colour associations and preferences in order to sell us their products. Packaging of products relies heavily on colour, both to carry information and to make the product attractive. Sugar, for example, is sold in packets coloured in bluey-pinks and blue because, unlike green, these colours are associated with sweetness. In experiments with washing powders, the colour of the packet has been shown to have a profound influence on choice. Even though the powder in three sample packets – coloured yellow, blue, and yellow-blue – was the same, customers thought the powder in the yellow packet was too strong, that in the blue packet too weak. The powder of choice was contained in the yellow-blue packet. In similar research, coffee in a brown can was thought to be too strong and in a red can too rich, in a blue can too mild and in a yellow can too weak – even though the coffee was the same in each case.

Fast-food outlets are often decorated with reds, yellows, and whites. Red makes the place warm and inviting, but also exciting so that it speeds the throughput of people. Yellow together with white emphasises hygiene. The combination creates a place where customers can relax and enjoy their food but do not linger too long.

The warm orange tones used in the colour scheme in this dining room (right) enhance the pleasure of entertaining friends for a meal.

Summary of colour effects

The chart on these two pages, based on the work of colour practitioners, indicates the effects of the predominant colours in a room. It will help you to analyse your current interior colour schemes as well as to plan any new ones. The details given in these guidelines apply to colours seen in daylight, or when full-spectrum lighting (see pp. 36-7) illuminates the room. Ordinary tungsten bulbs tend to add a yellowy–red appearance to the colours. Cool white fluorescent lighting also distorts colours, making them seem more blue.

Colour	Room	Use/Effect
RED	Use in activity areas, passages Not bedrooms, offices, factories, stress areas	Makes rooms look smaller Increases pulse rate Stimulates inhalation Keeps us alert Facilitates judgement Enhances activity Oppressive and tiring when dense and strong
ORANGE	Suitable for dining areas, entertainment areas, dancing halls, passages Not bedrooms, study, or stress areas	Stimulates and enhances dance and movement Encourages joyfulness, lightness, release, pleasure
YELLOW	Pure yellow is difficult to use; best in rooms to be used alone Not in offices, bedrooms, study, or work areas	Encourages detachment, nervousness and shallow breathing Suits mature minds
GREEN	For places that need balanced judgement, including operating theatres Not most living areas or activity areas	Promotes balance and careful judgement Makes rooms look flat, dead and empty Encourages indecision Arrests movement, encourages stasis
TURQUOISE	Kitchen, bathroom, bedrooms, offices, treatment rooms Not activity and play areas	Cool, refreshing, calming, soothing Good for nervous inflammation

Pale colours, often used in homes, have the same type of effect as their more colourful counterparts. The addition of white, however, tones down the impact. For example, strong blue will relax you almost to the point of sleep, while a pale blue is mildly relaxing; a strong red is overstimulating and therefore tiring, while pink is mildly stimulating and increases alertness.

Remember that paints are rarely pure in colour. Colours are mixed together and carry subtle tones that are not immediately apparent, but which nonetheless alter their effects.

Colour	Room	Use/Effect
BLUE	Bedrooms, offices, treatment rooms, stress areas Not dining rooms or entertainment areas	Calms, relaxes, creates feeling of breathing out, and sleep Helps to combat tension, asthmatic conditions, nervousness, and insomnia
VIOLET	Where dignity is necessary – entrance halls to hospitals, places of worship and dedication, also festive areas, lecture rooms Not in wards, or treatment rooms	Encourages purpose, prayer and meditation For dignity, reverance Calms body and balances mind
MAGENTA	Chapels, entrance halls, lecture rooms Not in entertainment areas	Colour of spiritual fulfilment Induces contentment, feeling of completeness, and self-respect
BLACK	Not suitable as an overall colour	Heightens emotional response
WHITE	A stark colour needing compensation with ornaments, paintings, plants, etc	Exaggerates purity Suggests a non-experience Gives stark effect

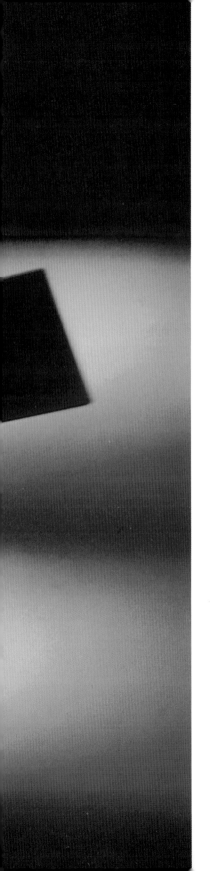

the science of colour

The immediate effects of the colour that surrounds you, both at home and at work, are easy to identify and use (see Chapter One). But a deeper understanding of the influence of colour and how colour can be used in therapy requires a closer look at how light brings colour into the body, and how the body registers colour messages.

How light enters the body

Our eyes are the most highly tuned of our organs for receiving coloured light. They supply about 90 per cent of the sensory information available to the brain. But information about light and colour also enters the body through the skin covering the whole surface of the body (see p. 20). Our eyes gather visual information, and channel it through to the brain so that we can perceive more accurately in consciousness what the body also experiences but does not make conscious (see pp. 48-9).

The physiology of light and colour detection via the eyes is well established (see *The pathways of light,* p. 20). Light passes through the lens at the front of each eye and registers on the retina at the back. Within the retina, specialized cells, known as cones, respond to the whole colour range, and these cells are at their most active during the day. As evening falls, a different set of light-sensitive cells, the rods, dominate vision. Although rods respond most readily to blue-green light they are sensitive to the intensity of light, whatever the colour. Rods are responsible for night vision. The rod and cone cells convert the light that enters the eye into electrical impulses, which the optic nerve then conveys to the back of the brain for interpretation.

Colour blindness

Some people are unable to register the difference between certain colours. Usually the difficulty is in distinguishing red from green, although other people cannot tell blue from yellow. About 8 per cent of men, and 1 per cent of women are red-green colour blind. But conscious sensitivity to certain colours bears no relation to the physiological effects of those wavelengths. Even when red and green are both seen as a muddy brown, each colour will have its different, specific effects on the body. As with visually impaired people, the impact of colour does not depend on being able to see. Perceptions of colour and light enter the body via the skin, even when clothed. All but the densest, darkest clothes allow light to penetrate. In this way, the predominant colours in the surroundings can still have their effect over the whole of the body.

History of colour science

Pythagoras, Plato, and Aristotle developed some of the early theories about light and sight. Pythagoras (c582 – c507BC) believed that objects themselves gave off particles that made them visible. Plato (427–347BC) thought that the eye emitted light, which bounced off objects, giving information on their shape, colour, and size. Aristotle (384–322BC) studied how light travels. His contribution was a theory that light travels in waves rather than particles. Aristotle's wave theory remains nearest to current thinking, but the wave versus particle argument raged for the next 2000 years, until physicists such as Max Planck (1858 – 1947) and Albert Einstein (1879 – 1955) laid the foundations for the currently accepted theory in the early years of the 20th century. Known as the "quantum" theory, it accepts elements of both the particle and the wave theories: light energy moves in discrete "packages", known as photons, and this movement may assume a wave form.

Isaac Newton (1642–1727) discovered that sunlight, although it appears to be white, is really a blend of colours. He performed a series of experiments in which he guided a shaft of sunlight through a glass prism in a darkened room so that the white light separated into its seven constituent colours – the colours of the rainbow.

Newton was a mathematician and philosopher before specializing in the science of optics, but like many men in the 17th century who were making discoveries at the forefront of science, he had a mystical side to his nature. He perceived seven colours in the spectrum (and seven is a mystical number). Goethe (1749 – 1832) identified six colours in the spectrum: three primary colours – red, yellow, blue – and three secondaries – orange, green, violet – the products of mixing the primaries. Goethe's reasoning came as much from his career as an artist as anything else: six colours served his practical purpose of mixing colours on a palette.

Wave energy

Electromagnetic waves have three features – wavelength, frequency (see p. 34), and amplitude. A wave with a short wavelength, such as ultraviolet light, has a high frequency and a great deal of energy. Amplitude is the height of the wave and gives a measure of its intensity, or brightness. Waves of large amplitude are brighter than waves of small amplitude.

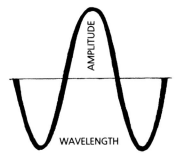

When a beam of white light is guided through each of four carefully placed prisms, (right), the coloured beams that emerge contain the eighth colour of the spectrum.

The number of colours in the spectrum is open to question: whether you see six, seven, or more depends on how exactly they are produced, how the overlapping colours appear, and what interpretation suits current theory!

Eight colours – including turquoise and magenta – are perceived by colour practitioners (see p. 40). Magenta can be seen very clearly when looking through a prism on to white paper printed with black lines or bars. The magenta comes out of this juxtaposition of black and white, which mixes red with violet light.

The electromagnetic spectrum

The universe is bathed in energy. During the births, lives, and deaths of stars, galaxies, and other astronomical bodies immense amounts of energy are produced. Cosmic rays, gamma radiation, X-rays, ultraviolet rays, visible light, infrared rays, microwaves, and radio waves – collectively called electromagnetic energy – fill the inner and outer reaches of the known universe. Whether they appear to behave as waves or particles (see p. 33) the various forms of electromagnetic energy have two features in common: they travel at the speed of light and are made up of an electrical component and a magnetic component, which vibrate at right angles to each other.

The electromagnetic spectrum
The electromagnetic spectrum (below), embraces energies from cosmic rays to radio waves. They are graded according to wavelength, measured in nanometres. One nanometre equals one millionth of a millimetre. The spectrum of visible light falls between 760nm at the violet end and 380nm at the red end.

For most purposes the energy can be considered as travelling in waves. The distance between successive waves is called the wavelength and the number of times a wave oscillates in one second is called the frequency. The rule of thumb is simple: the longer the wavelength of the energy, the lower the frequency.

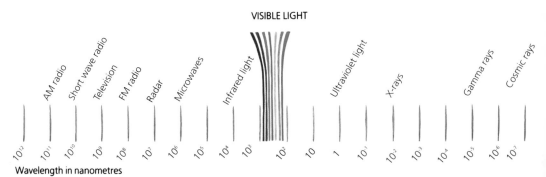

VISIBLE LIGHT

AM radio · Short wave radio · Television · FM radio · Radar · Microwaves · Infrared light · Ultraviolet light · X-rays · Gamma rays · Cosmic rays

10^{12} 10^{11} 10^{10} 10^{9} 10^{8} 10^{7} 10^{6} 10^{5} 10^{4} 10^{3} 10^{2} 10 1 10^{1} 10^{2} 10^{3} 10^{4} 10^{5} 10^{6} 10^{7}

Wavelength in nanometres

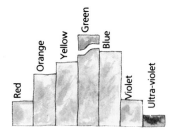

Daylight

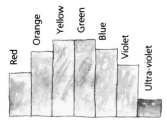

Fluorescent lamp
The spectrum of the light emitted from a fluorescent tube (above) is not full – there are more blues, greens, and ultraviolets than reds.

Full-spectrum lamp
The balance of the colours emitted by full-spectrum lamps (above) closely resembles daylight – reds, blues, and greens in roughly equal amounts.

All the forms of electromagnetic energy can be grouped into a spectrum (see p. 34). Cosmic rays have the shortest wavelength, the highest frequency, and the most energy. Consequently, they are the most damaging to living things. At the other end of the spectrum, radio waves have the longest wavelength, the lowest frequency, and the least energy.

Colour and wavelength

The narrow band of energy that the human eye can detect fits roughly into the middle of the electromagnetic spectrum. The wavelengths of this visible energy extend from about 380 nanometres at the red end to about 760 nanometres at the violet end. Each minute shift in wavelength within this band of energy can be sensed by our eyes and interpreted as a specific colour. In general, the colours are organized into the familiar visible spectrum – reds have the longest wavelengths, the lowest frequencies, and the least energy, while violets have the shortest wavelengths, the highest frequencies, and the most energy.

Beyond the red end of the visible spectrum there are the longer wavelengths of infrared radiation (which we feel as heat), microwaves (which we use in microwave ovens), and waves that we use for transmitting television and radio signals. Beyond the violet end there are the shorter wavelengths of ultraviolet radiation (which is essential for tanning the skin and for producing vitamin D in the body), X-rays, gamma rays, and cosmic rays.

Full-spectrum colour

The energy of sunlight produces all the wavelengths of colour, from ultraviolet through the visible spectrum to infrared, in a roughly even distribution. This is known as full-spectrum white light. We see the colour of an object when our eyes interpret the wavelengths of the light it reflects. For example, a blue vase will absorb all the component colours of the white light shining on it except the blue, which it reflects.

When illuminated by sunlight the grass and leaves of a garden in spring display a range of greens, from the light, yellowish tones of the young shoots to the darker shades of the more mature plants. The fact that each different green hue shares the same power and vibrancy indicates the full-spectrum quality of sunlight, in which all the green wavelengths are present in roughly equal amounts.

People who spend a great deal of time in artificial lighting, which does not emit the same balance of colours as sunlight, are depriving themselves of nourishment (see p. 20). Although they can see sufficiently well they may soon start to suffer from a deficiency of natural light. This is borne out by people suffering from a condition known as SAD – Seasonal Affective Disorder – which is a depression usually brought on by the lack of sunlight during winter. An excess of inadequate artificial lighting can bring on similar symptoms. However, full-spectrum lighting, often incorporating ultraviolet light, prevents the development of SAD.

Colour therapy lights are essentially full-spectrum lamps that are fitted behind coloured filters. These filters are made from quartz, and are coloured with gold, silver, or copper oxides to give a true, full-spectrum colour. Gold produces reds, silver creates sapphire blues, and copper can colour the quartz orange, yellow, blue, or turquoise. The filtered lights can thus produce colours of all the required wavelengths, frequencies, and energies. Ordinary artificial lights are unable to do this since they are more powerful in some wavelengths than in others. A cool white light, for instance, is weak in reds and violets, but strong in the colours between. When a red filter is placed in front of it, the resulting light is red but lacks the sufficient range of frequencies to be effective.

Extending the electromagnetic spectrum

Investigations into the mysteries of the universe have made scientists divide their subject matter into smaller and smaller parts. This goes against the elegant simplicity of the one world, one universe idea. However, recent advances in unified field theory have brought scientists back toward a more holistic approach to understanding phenomena.

Colour practitioners have developed a different view of the electromagnetic spectrum, by linking light, sound, and matter (see right). These are all manifestations of energy, some of which have electric and magnetic fields around them, and others that do not.

From darkness to form
In the extended electromagnetic spectrum high-energy, fast-vibrating cosmic rays emerge from the darkness, followed by gamma rays, X-rays, and so on through the spectrum to the slow-vibrating radio waves. Beyond these, the energy loses its electromagnetic qualities and emanates as sound. Eventually, the energy vibrates at the level of molecules and atoms – the realm of matter and form. The emergence from darkness of light, sound, and form can be plotted on the extended spectrum. Their positions are given by the proportions of the "golden mean" (see p. 38).

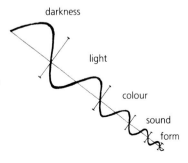

darkness

light

colour

sound

form

Just as music produces harmonic intervals, in which every note has a special relationship with each other, so all living things exhibit proportional relationships. Plants demonstrate these proportions clearly; look, for example, at the way a dandelion grows. Its leaves emerge from the centre with predictable spaces between them. The distances between these spaces are in the proportion of 1:1.6181, a proportion known as the "golden mean". In the early 13th century Fibonacci (c1170 – c1250), an Italian mathematician, recognized the "golden mean" relationship that was evident in plant, animal, and human structures and was the first to demonstrate this as a series of numbers, now known as the Fibonacci series (see Chapter Five). These patterns in nature are seen as evidence of the interrelationship of all forms of energy – whether visible or invisible.

Light and pigment

Colour practitioners use both coloured light and coloured objects in their treatments, although coloured light is more important because of its more powerful effect. Coloured lights and coloured pigments (in paints, dyes, etc) have different properties, based upon what happens when you mix

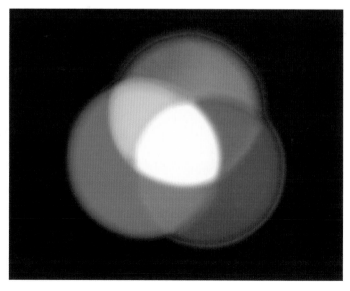

Red, green, and blue are the primary colours of light – if you mix them together in equal proportions you make white light. The colours of light are known as "additive", because they supply all the colours of the spectrum, which together make white. If you mix two primaries you make secondaries – red and green produces yellow, red and blue produces magenta, green and blue produces cyan (turquoise).

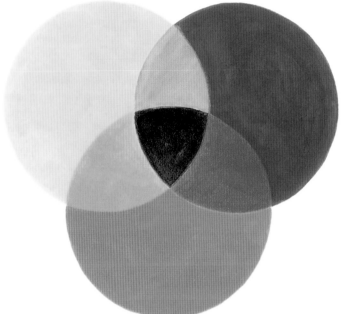

Mixing pigment colours

The primary colours of pigments, red, yellow, and blue, cannot be made by mixing any other colours. A mixture of these primaries looks black because together they absorb all the light that falls on them: a red pigment subtracts all the wavelengths from the light except red, which it reflects; a yellow pigment subtracts everything except yellow; a blue pigment subtracts everything except blue.

If you mix a pair of pigment primaries together you make the pigment secondaries – red and yellow make orange, red and blue make violet, yellow and blue make green.

Complementary colours

In the colour wheel (right) the eight colours of the spectrum all occur opposite their complementary colours (see p. 40). For example, turquoise is the complementary of red, and yellow is the complementary of violet.

To maintain the balance in the body that is essential for health, colours are always used in their complementary pairs in treatments (see Chapter Six).

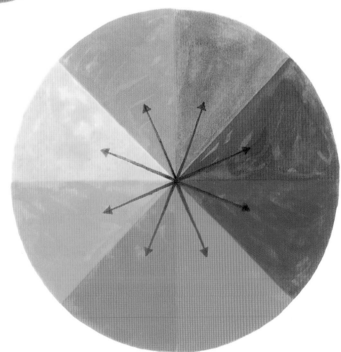

individual coloured lights or pigments together. Primary colours are those that cannot be made by mixing any other colours. The primary colours of pigment are different from those of light (see pp. 38-9).

Wholeness and complementary opposites

In general, we try to categorize all objects and beings in the world and, in so doing, lose the sense of wholeness from which everything springs. Only by coming to grips with where we belong, instead of emphasizing how different we are, will we regain this sense of wholeness.

Everything belongs with its opposite – the north and south poles of a magnet, male and female, light and dark, yin and yang. The two opposites, like two halves, complement each other and create a wholeness *(see right)*. Moreover, each half contains within it the potential for the other half. Thus, the male contains the female aspect; the darkness holds the potential of light within; the yang yearns for the yin.

A colour has its opposite, or complementary, too. Red and blue-green, yellow and violet, blue and orange are complementary pairs. But it is important to remember that every different hue has its complementary. The phenomenon of after-images illustrates complementary colours: if you stare at a red patch for about 30 seconds and then transfer your gaze to a white wall you will see a blue-green patch, the red's complementary. What is more, the quality of this after-image is a useful starting point for seeing colours in and around the body (see Chapter Four).

The importance of complementarity

One complementary colour enhances the colour of its opposite and when juxtaposed the pair makes the strongest contrast possible. Mixed together as light the two colours of a complementary pair balance each other and produce white. Thus, blue and orange light combine to make white light.

In the eight-colour spectrum of colour therapy, the complementary pairs are red and turquoise, orange and blue, yellow and violet, green and magenta *(see p. 39)*. Red, orange, and yellow are warm, magnetic colours, while turquoise, blue, and violet are cool, electric colours. Magenta and green are neutral in this respect. Complementarity is an

essential aspect of colour therapy. A healthy body contains complementary colours in equal proportions, so balanced colours denote a state of good health (see Chapter Four). If you treat an ailment with one colour without also using the balancing effect of its complementary you run the risk of making the ailment worse (see Chapter Six).

The interaction of opposites

In daylight, focus on the white circle in the centre of the diagram above. As you stare at it, you will see the interaction between the blue and white areas as they appear to move and become overlaid with the colours of the rainbow. The two opposites create the whole spectrum.

For a stronger effect, a photocopy of this page will give you the true opposites of black and white.

CHAPTER THREE

feeling the effects of colour

Human beings share their ability to respond to colour with the world around them (see p. 20). This similarity connects us to the rocks, minerals, vitamins, molecules, atoms – to all solids, liquids, and gases. All matter, both organic and inorganic, is sensitive to electromagnetic radiation at all frequencies, and thus all things respond to the electromagnetism of light, and to its constituent colours.

This chapter explores the ways in which we respond to colour – through the heart (intuition, emotion), the mind (brain, intellect), the body and its senses – and how we can enhance our colour sensitivity. It follows the path of all our experiences *(see below)*, which are met first by the emotional response generated by the heart – the seat of intuition (see

Feeling, thinking, and action

The diagram (right) *illustrates part of the infinite cycle of intuitive and intellectual responses that lead to physical action. Following the path from the left, the heart gives the first, emotional reaction, which is followed by the response of the intellect, represented here by a crown. The crown is a symbol of perfection and its use in this context reminds us that our thoughts are perfect, although they may not be translated into perfect actions.*

The intellect controls the response of the body, represented here by a square, the symbol of manifested energy.

Throughout the cycle the balance is maintained between the response of the heart, mind, and body.

pp. 100–1). Once we have made an emotional, intuitive response to a situation or encounter our intellect is activated by the brain. Our immediate response is analysed by the intellect, which controls the subsequent response of the whole body. In the philosophy of Rudolf Steiner, this pattern of responses is summarized as "feeling, thinking, willing".

By learning to listen to your intuitive response you will enhance your sensitivity to colour and maximize your colour experience. In other words, you will develop your potential for working with colour. You can strengthen your colour awareness through techniques such as visualization, breathing, and movement, and enhance your ability to bring individual colours into consciousness.

The intuitive knowledge of colour

Our first experience of colour takes place in the womb. Early in childhood, colour associations contribute to our consciousness. As we grow older we attach feelings, memories, and meanings to our experiences of colours, resulting in colour becoming a feature of our sub-conscious. The association of particular colours with a happy, sad, frightening, or some other experience builds up our colour preferences.

It is not too far-fetched to accept that our feelings about colour become so closely attached to the memories – events, people, places – that they form a framework that we use to look at the world. Our recollections and feelings are "coloured". They reflect our relationship with the outside world. Such is the basis of the psychology of colour. In the same way that each colour has physical and physiological implications for us all so, too, are there powerful psycho-logical, emotional, and spiritual connotations.

Our thoughts also colour our minds at an even deeper level. Our responses to colour are governed by deep-seated associations, which have been either conditioned by our experiences or inherited from our past. The phrase "I feel blue" indicates a cultural association between sadness and the colour blue; "seeing red" refers to the colour's deep-seated connection with anger. Expressions such as these indicate that we make intuitive connections between our feelings and the colours we use to describe them. Whether learned or inherited, the responses to colours are surprisingly similar the world over. This suggests the presence of universal colour associations that are part of our natural connection with our planet.

It is sometimes difficult to accept these intuitive thoughts; and because the practical aspects of life drown our ability to be quiet and thoughtful, they prevent our intuition from developing fully. In many ways, experience and learning override our intuition. If you want to deepen your consciousness of colour, the best way to begin is by relaxed contemplation, in which you are strongly aware of your feelings and in which you can trust your thoughts and find them valuable and worthwhile (see pp. 49-57). You can learn to heighten your intuitive response to encounters and experiences by allowing yourself the freedom to react to your initial feelings without analysing and substituting them with an intellectual response.

How shape enhances the power of colour

Colour practitioners work with colours that are presented in a particular form, or shape, because shape enhances the meaning of colour. The logical, left side of your brain focuses on the form, whereas the more creative, intuitive, right side responds to the emotional impact of colour itself.

By combining colour with particular shapes, you allow the right and left sides of your brain to work together, thus enabling your conscious and unconscious mind to respond as one. Each colour suggests its own shape – a shape that supports and maximizes the colour's own energy, and provides it with a natural container. The shape of each colour corresponds to the type of energy at work in the corresponding chakra *(see pp. 64-5)*. It also has internal energetic connections with the Platonic solids (see Chapter Five).

Colour and the senses

Each of your five senses transmits information about the outside world to your brain, which processes it for meaning and relays it to your conscious feelings. Each sense can enhance your colour experience but, equally, colour enhances the experience of the senses. Traditionally, each of the five senses is linked with a colour in a symbolic connection that has spiritual connotations.

Colour and form
Look at the colours on page 47, and focus on your feelings about each colour in the left-hand column. Then look at the right-hand column, where the colours are represented within a shape. Has the shape enhanced your feelings about the colour?

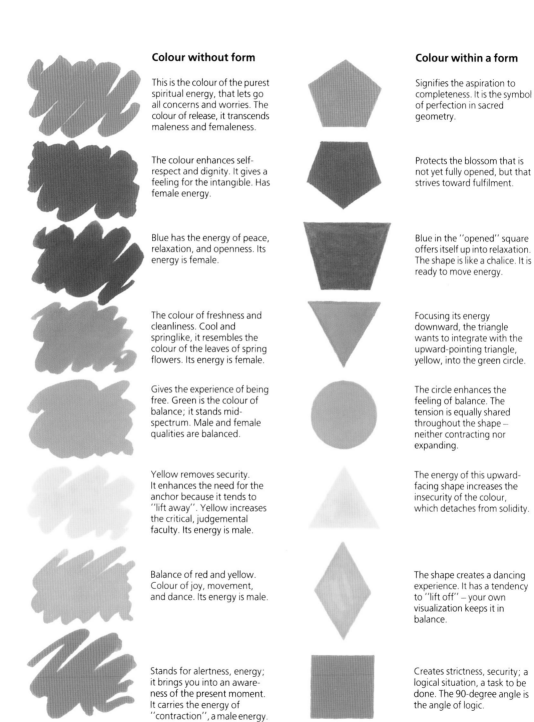

Colour without form

This is the colour of the purest spiritual energy, that lets go all concerns and worries. The colour of release, it transcends maleness and femaleness.

The colour enhances self-respect and dignity. It gives a feeling for the intangible. Has female energy.

Blue has the energy of peace, relaxation, and openness. Its energy is female.

The colour of freshness and cleanliness. Cool and springlike, it resembles the colour of the leaves of spring flowers. Its energy is female.

Gives the experience of being free. Green is the colour of balance; it stands mid-spectrum. Male and female qualities are balanced.

Yellow removes security. It enhances the need for the anchor because it tends to "lift away". Yellow increases the critical, judgemental faculty. Its energy is male.

Balance of red and yellow. Colour of joy, movement, and dance. Its energy is male.

Stands for alertness, energy; it brings you into an aware-ness of the present moment. It carries the energy of "contraction", a male energy.

Colour within a form

Signifies the aspiration to completeness. It is the symbol of perfection in sacred geometry.

Protects the blossom that is not yet fully opened, but that strives toward fulfilment.

Blue in the "opened" square offers itself up into relaxation. The shape is like a chalice. It is ready to move energy.

Focusing its energy downward, the triangle wants to integrate with the upward-pointing triangle, yellow, into the green circle.

The circle enhances the feeling of balance. The tension is equally shared throughout the shape – neither contracting nor expanding.

The energy of this upward-facing shape increases the insecurity of the colour, which detaches from solidity.

The shape creates a dancing experience. It has a tendency to "lift off" – your own visualization keeps it in balance.

Creates strictness, security; a logical situation, a task to be done. The 90-degree angle is the angle of logic.

Sense	Colour	Zodiac Sign	Gem	Element
Sight	Red	Aries	Onyx	Fire
Hearing	Yellow	Gemini	Gold topaz	Air
Smell	Green	Aquarius	Ruby	Water
Taste	Blue	Pisces	Sapphire	Earth
Touch	Violet	Libra	Aquamarine	Ether

Sight

Of all the senses, sight enhances your colour awareness most. Its predominant effect takes place at the physical level, which is associated with the colour red. Red helps you "pull yourself together" by enhancing your awareness of the "here and now". Generally, red has a contracting effect: "seeing red" refers to the very contracted or tense state of anger.

Hearing

By closing your eyes you remove the powerful sense of sight and enhance your powers of hearing. This helps to increase your awareness of colour images produced by the sounds of music and speech. Equally, your most intense colour sensations can make their presence felt as sounds. Sound can "shed light" on an experience, and allows the intellect to let go of ideas generated through sight. Hearing is associated with the element of air and the colour yellow. This colour symbolism illustrates the beginnings of traditional colour connections between ourselves, the elements, and the energies of the planet.

Smell

Scents and smells indicate that a change is taking place. They are generated either when energies interact or when a chemical change occurs. The sense of smell is associated with the colour green, the point of balance as the change takes place. The fact that the olfactory region of the brain is one of the first parts of the brain to evolve explains, at least in part, why smells can trigger strong memories and evoke early experiences of colour associations.

Using sound to enhance light

The link between colour and sound was familiar to the Druids who, at the winter solstice, retreated to their caves for three days. On the third day, each cave would be flooded with light and sound that seemed to have no source. By chanting, the Druids produced the full spectrum of harmonic overtones, which created a state of awareness that "let in" the full spectrum of light.

Taste

The experience of tasting delicious food or the full flavours of a drink is expansive – it takes you over and makes you vulnerable to the sensations. The expansiveness is associated with the colour blue, the colour that makes you relax. Blue acts as a taste enhancer when used to solarize water (see p. 116) – water in a blue glass (or a glass with a blue filter around it), left in sunlight for as little as 30 to 45 minutes will taste sweeter than before!

Touch

Your hands can heal by conveying more than the sense of touch – touching with care gives dignity, an invisible energy associated with spirituality. Because of this link with a higher level of consciousness, the sense of touch is associated with the colour violet. Visually impaired people can interpret colours through feeling the density and temperature of the air that surrounds objects. By this "touch at a distance" people with poor sight can live in a world of colour.

If you visualize violet when giving someone a massage, for example, you will help that person feel uplifted. By making colour part of the whole experience you will improve the quality of your touch.

Enhancing your responses to colour

Equipped with an awareness of your heart, mind, and body responses to colour, and the knowledge that all your senses contribute to your colour perception, you are ready to embark upon the practical techniques for enhancing your colour feelings. The visualization, breathing, and movement exercises that follow on pages 50 to 57 will prepare you for working with the healing power of colour, as well as guide you into the specific healing uses of the techniques that are described in the chart on page 101.

As a preliminary step in this process you should intensify your exposure to colour and heighten your responses to it. To begin, try the exercise described on the following page. Talk about a particular colour with a group of friends or fellow students. By identifying and strengthening your colour associations you will become more aware of the characteristics of individual colours and begin to notice how they change the way you feel.

Talking about colours

Red and blue are the best colours to discuss first because their effects are so different and our experiences of them are often clear and plentiful. Sit in a circle and begin by describing the colour red. You do not need to see the colour, just keep it in your mind and let it "sink into you" as you speak. Then focus on your wider associations with the colour, recounting your

experiences and feelings briefly. Listen to the rest of the group expressing their feelings about the colour and take in their thoughts.

After a few minutes you will notice that speech speeds up and the group members become more tense, as if anxious and on edge. Their breathing becomes more shallow and people generally feel ill at ease.

Talking about blue produces the opposite effect, almost one of lethargy. The members of the group speak more slowly and their breathing becomes deeper and slower. Examples of individual associations with the colour take longer to emerge. Time seems to pass more slowly and eventually the group runs out of energy for the discussion.

Colour visualization

The technique of colour visualization enables you to continue the enhancement of your colour sensitivity. You can then combine it with colour breathing exercises (see p. 54) and finally with movements that help you to express the feelings associated with the different colours (see pp. 56-7). The end result will give you an intimacy with colour that will not only prepare you for seeing a person's aura (see Chapter Four) but will also enable you to feel and work with the energy of individual colours for specific healing purposes (see Chapter Six).

In general, using your mind's eye for visualization helps you to balance negative thoughts – those that have lingered in your mind for many years tend to increase the ageing process because of the chronic tensions they produce. As a rule, use visualizations to accentuate positive feelings – use images of what you want to happen, rather than what you fear might happen.

The colour red, in all its shades, from deepest crimson to palest pink, represents strength and vitality, and is energizing and stimulating. A red rose (right) is the symbol of emotional and physical love.

Visualization might be difficult to start with because it makes you feel awkward and the images are cluttered up with everyday thoughts. Use the simple relaxation (see p. 53) as a preparation for your colour visualization. This enhances your concentration and enables you to focus more clearly on the images. Being relaxed also has the advantage of allowing your body to absorb colour readily, and this contributes toward the healing process.

Simple relaxation

Lie on your back on the floor. Make sure that your body is straight and your chin tucked in. Your legs should be slightly apart and your hands by your sides, palms facing upward.

Relax your mind, and let any thoughts float up into the atmosphere like beautiful balloons, and then gently disperse. Then bring your concentration into your body. Starting with your head, use your mind to work down your body to your feet.

Gently let go of any tension and feel yourself starting to relax.

Then, on the next inhalation, bring your arms up over your head and stretch your whole body.

Exhaling, bring your arms down to your sides. Repeat this twice: Now gently roll on to your side and sit up.

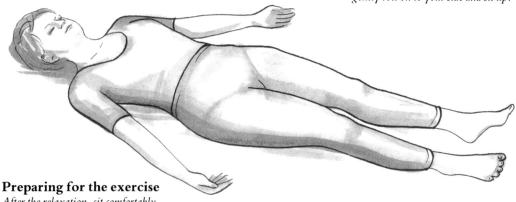

Preparing for the exercise

After the relaxation, sit comfortably, and follow the simple visualization exercise given below. You can work with any colours for this exercise (see p. 54). The example below describes a visualization using blue, and its complementary, orange.

Simple visualization

Exhale slowly and close your eyes. Inhale gently, and imagine that you are sitting by a blue lake. The sky is blue above you. As you exhale, think of looking at the intense orange of a large marigold flower. Feel the calmness of the blue fill your body.

Repeat the exercise a few times, then sit quietly for a few moments before you get up. The breathing technique is described in more detail on page 54.

Visualization-meditation

To take colour visualization a stage further you can meditate upon an inner story. An example of such a story is told on page 53. Familiarize yourself with it or ask a friend to read it to you. Alternatively, imagine a story of your own.

Think of this visualization as a way of travelling "out of your body". Before starting, you must feel assured that you can return safely. To do this, relax (see above) and sit upright, then look at the space around you. Remember the colours and shapes that you see. Feel protected by the space, and ready to return there after your visualization.

Exhale slowly, close your eyes, and follow the story below in your mind's eye.

At the end of the story, take a deep breath and bring your thoughts back into your body. Return to the vision of yourself as you were before closing your eyes.

Finally, imagine a ring of light that contains a cross of light. Think of your eight chakras (see p. 65) and, starting from the top – the crown chakra – visualize the ring and cross of light working as a golden key to "close" each chakra in turn. This protects you from the shock of re-entering your normal consciousness.

The inner story

I walk into a market place on a sunny afternoon. It seems strangely empty and no one seems to see me.

I am drawn to the church at the end of the square. The door leads down into a deep crypt where the red eternal flame burns in front of an altar. I let this red flame take me inside its strength, even power, and remain there experiencing this feeling of life-giving energy. The image of God the Father comes to mind.

After a while I stand up and walk up a few steps to a hall where the light is orange. Many people are dancing, moving. There is joy and laughter. I am only an onlooker and no one acknowledges my presence.

A flight of stairs leads me up into the main aisle of the church. The vaults reflect a yellow light; all seems so detached; it feels lonely, almost empty; I can't stay there long and I look for an exit.

Behind the altar a door leads into a grassy field. The green restores my balance and I walk on the grass toward a forest.

The colour under the leaves of the trees is turquoise: fresh, pure, and making me immune from any kind of influence. It feels as if everything is just beginning.

I walk through this forest and stand before a blue lake. Some blue hills across the water give me peace. I am relaxed and very calm.

As I look across the lake, a beautiful being bathed in a violet light moves toward me. I am overcome with a dignity I have not experienced before. In its hands burns a beautiful magenta flame. This flame is free and lets go of all density or substance.

The figure does not change in size as it comes toward me. The violet and magenta increase in strength and uplift me, filling me with respect, not just for this being but also for myself. Now it stands before me and speaks in a clear and beautiful language: "You are to take this light and carry it in your heart; it is the light of pure love. Let go of all past burdens."

As I accept this light, naturally and without hesitation, it is still in the hands of this being whom I recognize as my higher self – pure, free of burden, and just complete love. There are no strings attached to this love – only love. "Take this light into your everyday life and give it to all you meet." The being (and it feels as if it is myself giving myself the permission to go back into the world) retreats across the lake and I am nevertheless aware that it is also with me at my own calling. The words "World without end," sound within me.

The flame in my hands penetrates the blue of the lake and shares this cool, relaxing peace. I walk back through the forest – the trees and shrubs smile as I give them my flame of love, the flame of magenta. It is a very pure, very light magenta, almost white. I am not alone any more. The grasses, the little flowers, the rabbits come to me as I cross the green field.

I did not notice all this before. I return to the church; the yellow arches are still detached but they shine now as if they were golden and absorb my flame of light. I descend into the orange hall and offer my flame of pure magenta to the people who come to me. Each one now has one flame also. I say to them: "Share it always, share it or else it will go out." To be joyful and dancing with the light of love seems so natural.

And now I descend into the crypt, where I can accept the red of the life energy, which resides in the base of our being, through which we can create the future children to maintain the Earth and its life. I suddenly realize that my magenta flame of love is not only in my hands but penetrates all the cells of my body; nothing is untouched by this flame of love.

Humble yet proud, I ascend the stairs and enter the market place, which is busy with many stalls. I go to each stall holder and give them my light of love. I had not noticed until now that the light in my hands is only the centre of a vast radiance all around me and that as I give it away it radiates even stronger each time I share it.

Now slowly return to your normal waking state, (see left) using a deep breath, and closing your chakras.

The calmness that comes from meditation on the blue of water beneath a blue sky (right) can be experienced through the simple visualization on page 52.

Colour breathing

Breathing does more than bring oxygen into your body and remove the carbon dioxide from your blood; it sustains and revitalizes your spiritual energy. Your breathing provides a continual interaction with the world around you. Concentrating on your breath also allows you to clear your mind of unwanted thoughts. Furthermore, rhythmic and stable breathing provides you with a firm platform from which to explore your conscious and subconscious self. Breathe fully, and rhythmically, from deep inside your abdomen.

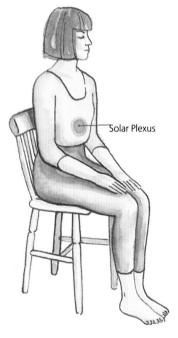

Solar Plexus

Simple breathing technique

Lie down, or sit up with your spine relaxed and straight. Breathe at a rate that is comfortable for you. Do not try to elongate the inward and outward breath and do not hold your breath. Just establish a natural rhythm, focusing on the breath until your mind is calm, and free of unwanted thoughts.

In your mind's eye hold a positive image of yourself; for example, picture yourself at a time when you felt particularly well or happy. Now bring a colour to mind.

You can either go through the whole spectrum of colours, or choose a particular one for its healing qualities (see right).

When you have decided on your colour, breathe in, visualizing the colour entering your solar plexus and spreading throughout your body just beneath the skin. If you wish, imagine the colour penetrating a specific part of your body. As you breathe out, visualize the complementary colour. Use the information that follows to guide your colour choices.

Red *Breathe in red for vitality. It brings energy and increases sexuality, strength, and will power. Breathe out turquoise.*

Orange *Breathe in orange for joy, happiness, and fun. Breathe out blue.*

Yellow *Breathe in yellow to increase your objectivity and intellectual powers. Breathe out violet.*

Green *Breathe in green to cleanse, to feel more balanced, and to combat tumours. Breathe out magenta.*

Turquoise *Breathe in turquoise to counteract inflammations and fever, to strengthen the immune system. Breathe out red.*

Blue *Breathe in blue for relaxation and peace, and in cases of sleeplessness. Breathe out orange.*

Violet *Breathe in violet to increase self respect, and for feelings of dignity and beauty. Breathe out yellow.*

Magenta *Breathe in magenta to let go of any obsessional images, thoughts, and reminiscences. Breathe out green.*

Movement

The beautiful gestures of eurythmy introduced by Rudolf Steiner at the beginning of the 20th century provide a series of simple movements that help your colour visualization. Eurythmy was developed as a performance art, but has a therapeutic use, and can be practised in order to enhance the feelings associated with each colour.

The movements developed from the contrasting feelings associated with "light" and "dark". Yellow is the lightest colour in the spectrum, and the colour most like the sun. The position that represents this light is very open, with the arms reaching up, as if toward the sun. Conversely, the darkest colour, indigo, is characterized by the arms held low, and the body folded downward. Between these extremes the characteristics of each colour style the position. Eurythmy always involves movement that follows the shapes already made by the body, so none of the colour positions is static. You pursue the colour's form by following it through; and moving the arms.

Moving from light to dark

Begin by lifting your arms up and slightly to the sides. Relax your chest and keep it "open", as if to receive the light (see position 1, right). Then bend one knee, lifting your heel to help the movement. Let your knee curl in toward the other leg. As you do this, fold your body forward, relax your arms and lower them as much as you can, gently closing them across your body, as if shutting out the light. This position represents dark blue, the colour of darkness (see position 2, far right).

Position 1   Position 2

Red

Red is much darker than yellow, but contains more activity. From position 1, dip your hands down in front of you, then push them up briskly but smoothly in front of your face. The colour red is a very dynamic colour and the movement is correspondingly fast and firm. Its movement is "penetrating", sometimes almost aggressive. It helps you "cut through" any problems.

Green

Green is the colour between yellow and blue in the spectrum of colours. The movement explores the middle region, with the hands held out to the side. Maintain the height of your arms as you move them around, and step both in straight lines and circular shapes, reflecting the balance between "open" and "closed" movements.

Yellow

Yellow is the brightest colour of the spectrum, but not as brilliant as white light. So, from position 1, lower one arm very slightly forward, and think of it as a shaft of light. Lower your other arm down behind you, completing the diagonal with the arm that faces up. Move gracefully forward and back in straight lines, following the diagonal direction of your arms.

For colours that are made from a combination of two others – orange, for example, contains red and yellow, and violet is made of red and blue – the position of the arm and the movement of the body should reflect the characteristics of both. As you move, the extreme positions of each colour "give up" something of themselves, to produce a flowing movement of a single colour.

CHAPTER FOUR

colour energies in the body

This chapter focuses attention on the subtle colour energies that surround your body all the time but usually go unnoticed. More than that, it looks at how energy emanates from your body itself. And it shows how you can begin to learn to perceive this energy as a colour signal, which is a direct indication of the health of both body and mind.

A cautionary note is called for here. From the information in this chapter you can learn only how to start to increase your colour perception. In order to see colour images with absolute clarity, you have to use techniques that involve going into deep meditational states that alter your brainwave patterns. For this you need the instruction and direct supervision of a qualified practitioner. You can, however, practise the techniques of dowsing described here (see p. 70), in order to detect the colour energies of the spine. This will give you an introduction to experiencing colour energy and prepare you for further guidance.

Energy input and output

The energy we need for life comes not only from our food and drink but also from the electromagnetic radiations of the sun, and the invisible forces of galactic space. The effect of the moon, alone, is greater than you might think. Its gravitational influence over the tides is well documented; less well known is the fact that some surgeons are cautious about performing surgery around the time of the full moon, because of the moon's tidal impact on the flow of blood in the body.

We do not find it difficult to think of plants drawing on sunlight in the process of photosynthesis, using the energy from the rays that penetrate their leaves to combine the carbon dioxide from the air with the water and trace elements drawn up from the earth, and so to produce the material for growth and reproduction. In this process, the sunlight energy is necessary to the plant for the synthesis of food.

We human beings are also bathed in light from the sun, which affects our bodies directly. The light penetrates our skin and muscles, even our skull (see p. 20), to bring warmth and produce chemical changes in body tissues. It also triggers hormonal effects that alter the pattern of our growth and reproductive processes. Thus there is an essential interaction between ourselves and the energy that surrounds us.

Haloes and wings
Familiar "halo" shapes traditionally surround the heads of Jesus and the saints in paintings during the time of Fra Angelico and Botticelli in the 15th century, and other Italian artists dating back to the 12th and 13th centuries and before. These, and the wings of angels, are an historic acknowledgement of the perception of more than just the physical human form.

The halo and wings are not, however, the prerogative of saints and angels. They are potentially present in the auras of all humans.

Everything on earth takes energy in, and releases energy. The process of life and growth involves this exchange of energy with the environment – an input and an output. Part of the output is a unique energy field that exists around every living being, including human beings. Think of a human being as having not only the immediately visible physical body, but emanations of this subtle "output energy" that surround the body, but are not visible (or only visible to some). They form a protective zone of transition between your physical body and the outside world. This area is called an aura. It holds your life energy, reflects your state of health, and filters out and takes in the energies of the universe. The aura is continually moving and pulsing, and this free movement of energy is what keeps you healthy (see also Chapter Five).

Minerals, plants, animals, and humans all have their own auras, which differ in their complexity and colour ranges (see *Evolution of the aura, below*). Minerals have a white aura around them, plants a golden one, while the aura surrounding animals is indigo blue. That of humans is multi-layered, and multi-coloured. This complexity represents the added dimension of consciousness, together with all aspects of our physical, mental, emotional, and spiritual functioning; it is expressed in eight (or possibly more) subtle layers (see pp. 62-3). The vibrations and colours of the layers of a human aura alter as a result of internal changes in health and consciousness and the effects of external energies (see pp. 76-7), although the overall shape of the aura remains more or less constant. These are natural phenomena, indicating the normal changes that take place in healthy, living things.

Evolution of the aura

Before the existence of matter, there was darkness. Then a slowing, or contraction of cosmic energies yielded light energy. As it slowed, it produced colour, then contracted into sound, and finally into matter (see p. 37). Where the energies contracted very quickly, they formed dense, solid matter, such as minerals and crystals; those energies that "drew in" more slowly gave rise to living matter – cells, plants, animals, and finally produced favourable conditions for the emergence of human life.

All matter releases energy. Matter that was formed by a quick contraction of energy releases its condensed energy very slowly. Dense, solid objects have still auras, which are difficult to perceive. Human auras are mobile and fluctuating.

Structure of the aura

Immediately surrounding our physical self is an etheric sheath, extending three to four inches (8-10 cm) around the body and following its form. It is the spiritual blueprint from which the physical body develops. Under normal conditions its colour is a very pale magenta (it is absolutely white when the person is spiritually highly evolved). Those who communicate in a peaceful and relaxed manner produce a bluish energy that colours the sheath. Good teachers are surrounded by a cobalt blue etheric sheath. A violet note suggests someone with dignity, who may, therefore, be involved in religious work.

Around the etheric sheath is the aura itself, a three-dimensional ovoid extending several feet in all directions, in volume about 22 times larger than the human form. The aura contains layers of colour just like the rainbow and these layers are continuously moving, interpenetrating each other with their clear, pure colour. These movements respond to environmental inputs as well as shifts in thought, feeling, and physical wellbeing. The layers of the aura are a pre-manifestation of the whole person. ·Each corresponds to a different aspect of the human function.

The human aura

The first layer, next to the etheric sheath, is **red.** Red is the densest colour and relates to the physical body and sexuality. The **orange** layer, next to it, is the energy of the life force, the metabolic body. These two layers are very closely linked. The metabolic body maintains the physical body during sleep and provides the energies of breathing, heartbeat, and blood circulation. It also nourishes the involuntary nervous system. It is sometimes referred to as the etheric body. The **yellow** layer, also known as the astral body, corresponds to the solar plexus and the emotional energies: the soul of the individual. Next to yellow is the **green** layer, representing the ego, personality, and the capacity to think and make connections between the physical individual and the subtle, finer, spiritual energies of the aura. Green is the colour of balance; this is the area of exchange between the ego and the higher self. The **turquoise** layer that follows the green links up with the higher mental, or super-mental, inspirational self. The **blue** layer is the model for the causal body, or motivation; it holds

The human aura

The aura extends all around every human being (facing page). Always in a state of flux, its size, shape, and colour depend on the precise condition of the individual. To those people who are gifted and those with special training, the aura is easily perceived, and so can be used in colour therapy, providing a useful diagnostic device and a guide to treatment.

Quality of colours in the aura

The colours of the aura are clear and luminous; they are indescribably fine emanations of energy.

You can see for yourself what this special quality of light is like by looking at a solid printed colour for about 15 seconds, in order to saturate your vision. Then cover the colour with an opaque sheet of white paper. The new colour that you see now – which is the complementary colour to the original – has a luminescent quality. This is similar to the quality of colour that is visible in the aura.

Sharing an aura

The shape and size of your aura depends on your feelings and your state of health. When you meet a real friend, you feel warm and "expansive" – and your aura grows accordingly. The opposite happens when you meet someone you dislike; your aura contracts and "withdraws". If you are both in the expansive state, you each move into the other's aura, absorbing its energies and, to some extent, leaving the imprint of your own aura there.

in it the plan for life that we would ideally love to live. Beyond this is the **violet** layer – the higher self, the bodyless body, the true essence, and the greater consciousness. The last layer that is discernible is the **magenta,** representing the spirit self, the identity, the eternal being.

Chakras

The auric layers are "breathing" energies around the human being that correspond to living energy. By contrast, there is another energy comparable to rays of light, shining both into and out of centres in the body. These centres are known as the "chakras". Sanskrit teachings from Tibet well over 2000 years ago talked of three chakras. Later, the Tibetans recognized five, and since then seven and more have been acknowledged. Eight chakras, corresponding to the eight colours of the aura, are described below.

The chakras are lens-like structures that collect and strengthen the light that surrounds us. Each chakra has a greater and lesser centre (see p. 65). Whereas the layers of the aura that surround the human body produce a "container" energy, the chakras provide the "content" of the container. These two energies are complementary, and work together both to create and to maintain life. The container energy of the aura is the feminine aspect and the ray-like chakra energy provides the masculine aspect of these complementary energies.

The colours and functions of chakras

Magenta The crown chakra relates to the pineal gland. Magenta is the colour of the eternal, spiritual self, made up of the energies of perfection. The centre of spirituality, this chakra connects you to an infinite intelligence.	**Violet** The brow chakra, also known as the third eye, transmits the energy of the pituitary gland. Known in yoga as the 1000-petalled lotus flower, it is the centre of creative visualization, and gathers instruction from your higher self.	**Blue** The third, throat chakra is centred at the energy of the thyroid gland. It is the centre for creative expression through sound, and as such is significant in matters of communication and truth.	**Turquoise** The chakra of the thymus gland is very closely linked with the heart, and connected with a generosity of life and love.
Green The heart chakra is the centre of love and harmony. This is the area for a person's soul to shine through. Green is the colour of balance.	**Yellow** The solar plexus, like a sun, is the light that has descended into the nervous system. From here you are sensitive to situations. It is the centre of human recognition and self worth. Unresolved situations create stress here.	**Orange** The sacral chakra relates to the adrenal glands, and is strongly influenced by genetic patterning. Its connection is less spiritual, more earthly. Physical movement, wellbeing, and joy relate to this chakra.	**Red** The base chakra is connected to passion, life energy, sexuality, and the power to create.

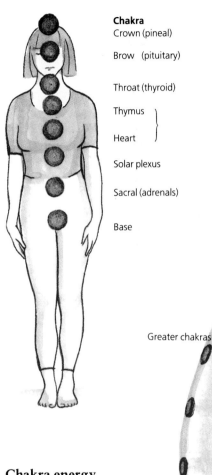

Chakra	Sanskrit name
Crown (pineal)	Sahasrara
Brow (pituitary)	Ajna
Throat (thyroid)	Vishudda
Thymus ⎫ Heart ⎭	Anahata
Solar plexus	Manipura
Sacral (adrenals)	Swadisthana
Base	Muladhara

The chakras

The eight chakras, corresponding to the eight coloured layers of the aura, lie in line with the spine, in the etheric sheath (see below).

Traditionally in Tibetan teaching the thymus and heart are one energy, so these two chakras share the common Sanskrit name.

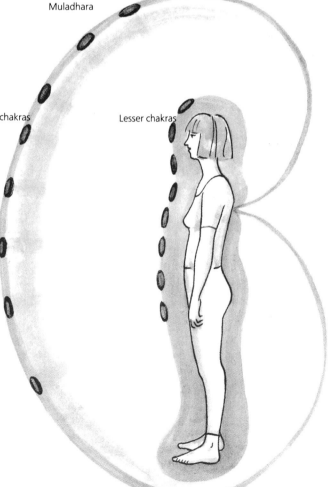

Greater chakras   Lesser chakras

Chakra energy

From the side, the energies surrounding the body produce a kidney-shaped profile. A funnel of energy, even finer and more transparent than the aura, penetrates to the 5th thoracic vertebra, at the level of the heart. This is where the energy of light guides each individual along the way.

The position of the smaller, or "lesser" chakras corresponds to the edge of the etheric sheath, about 3½ – 4ins (9-10cm) from the body. The greater chakras are at the edge of the aura, about 32ins (45cm) from the body.

Detecting colour energies

Early attempts to measure and detect aura and chakra energies were made in the late 19th and the first half of the 20th centuries. This interest was a response to technical advances, including the early use of electrotherapy, and to claims by scientists and clairvoyants who reported seeing luminous emanations surrounding the body.

Walter John Kilner was a physician and surgeon at St Thomas' Hospital, London. After his appointment in 1869, he became director of the one of the first X-ray departments. His attempts to design an instrument that would allow him to see the luminous emanations of the body led to experiments with a dye known as dicyanin. By looking through a lens coated with the dye, he could perceive light in the ultraviolet range. The apparatus became known as the Kilner screen, and it made visible a blue-grey band of light that extended six to eight inches (15-20cm) around the body, with a second band of almost vaporous light extending outward. He found that fatigue, disease, or mood could alter the size and colour of the radiation. Magnetism, electricity, and hypnosis also altered the image.

In the 1930s and 1940s, a Russian technician, Semyon Kirlian, observed tiny flashes of light on the skin of patients receiving electrotherapy. He devised equipment to reproduce this effect and recorded the result on photographic paper. One of his most significant findings was that every person produces a unique energy pattern.

Human potential

These attempts to measure invisible human energy patterns, to a large extent the product of their age, made important advances in the acceptability of the idea of the human aura. But no instrument has been able to detect more of the aura than the etheric energy that immediately surrounds the body. Human beings, however, have the potential ability to perceive the multi-coloured human aura directly. The pituitary gland is thought to be the organ responsible for this perception. A few people retain the gift from birth, but most lose it. Colour practitioners receive training in how to become aware of auras and to dowse for colour in the body. They may use any of the techniques described on the pages that follow.

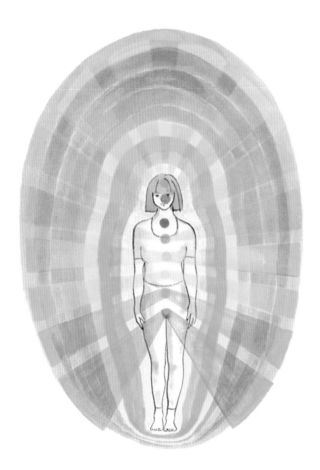

Energy in the aura and the chakras

The human aura is three-dimensional, surrounding the body in all directions (see p. 62). Similarly the energies surrounding the body that funnel into the chakras come from all directions (see p. 65).

In this two-dimensional representation, the aura is shown flat on the page, while the chakra energies are focused in from above the page. Where the chakra energy shines directly into the aura the colours of the chakra energies and the layers of the aura mingle, creating pure and luminous colours.

Perceiving auras

Learning to become aware of auras involves voluntary and controlled changes in brain states. You can start to learn the techniques for perceiving auras yourself (see pp. 68-70), though a good teacher will always be your best guide. The techniques are simple, and closely connected with the relaxation exercise described on page 53. But you will need guidance in returning from such altered brain states. They should not be attempted on your own.

Altered brain states

You, as a human being, are able to change your brain state at will. The following description gives you an idea of the different levels of brainwave patterns that you can achieve, and which you need to experience in order to become conscious

Accepting colour energies

Start by thinking about the colours, and accept the possibility that you, too, can perceive them. Imagine perceiving the colours of the aura. Allow the subtle energies into your consciousness. If you can do this without feeling that you are "pretending" to experience the colours, you will probably start to become aware of colour sensation. Not necessarily immediately; it will be easier for some than for others. But once you have really accepted the possibility, you become more receptive to the colour energies. Go back to the exercise on page 40; and remember that the quality of the colours is transparent and luminous. Practise the exercise until you have seen the whole range of complementary colours with the same luminous quality as an aura. After that, it is a matter of letting these colours in; allow yourself to see them, and these subtle energetic vibrations can become clear to you.

of the colours of the aura. Four levels of brain activity are described here, all of which can be recorded on an electro-encephalograph. The brainwaves become longer as the brain pulse decreases. These changing levels of consciousness can be accessed through meditation, which makes an excellent and safe introduction to altering the pulse rate of the brain.

Slowing the brainwaves

In an anxious state, mental activity can reach 34 cycles per second – the *higher beta* rate. The brain pulse rate during normal human activity is 21 cycles per second, the speed of the normal *beta* rhythm. The level below *beta* is the calm *alpha* state, at 13 cycles per second. This alpha state is the natural level of brain pulse rate for animals.

Below *alpha* is the *seta* state, when your brain is slowed to about 8 cycles per second, and you are even more focused and calm. At this point solid objects start to look transparent. If you slow your brain one stage further, to 5 cycles per second, you are in the *delta* state. You can no longer differentiate between hearing, seeing, and feeling. Time and space become interchangeable. You can at once feel an experience and "see" it as if you were on the outside. Perception no longer depends on the "sight". In this state you need help to be drawn back into more normal states of consciousness.

Consciousness and your aura

The change in your consciousness is also reflected in your own aura. The normal, *beta* pulse rate produces the typical multi-coloured aura. As your rate slows to *alpha*, the aura shows a blue overlay. At *seta*, the blue gives way to gold, and if the *delta* state is reached, the aura is almost white, lightly tinged with magenta. In effect, you are moving through all the levels of consciousness of the evolutionary process (see p. 61).

The aim is to slow the brain pulses. This has the effect of finely tuning your perception to the higher vibration level of colour energies. As your brain pulse slows, you become more receptive than in your normal brain state.

As a result of moving into a meditative state some people suddenly find themselves able to "see" what they previously could not. This can also happen as the result of a shock – whether good or bad – which detaches your personality and soul from your physical self. In this detached state, you are open to "seeing" things that you would not normally see. By being more "opened up" to the energy of light, you allow its colours to influence you.

Asking permission

Looking into someone's aura is a very personal matter. Always ask permission before entering into this world of subtle messages. You may well experience a distorted image if you go into it without permission.

Colour in the spine

The aura and the chakra system are two ways of expressing the presence of colour energies in and around the body. A third way of looking at these energies is as they might appear in the spine. It is possible to look at the spine of the human structure as carrying within it a memory of its own stages of evolution.

This process is recorded as deep-seated memory within the spine and the nervous system. The vertebrae, which house the central cord of this system, and the skull, can be divided into five sections, each representing one of these evolutionary stages; the physical manifestation, the metabolic processes, the emotions, the intellect, and the spirituality. Each section contains eight vertebrae, each with the concentrated colour energies of the eight colours of the spectrum (see p. 71).

Sensing colours in the spine

If you have not yet experienced the ability to "see" the colours that surround people, you can tune your senses to the vibrations of colour through dowsing. The most well known style of dowsing is with a water diviner, a forked stick that helps to concentrate the energies below ground level. The pendulum is almost as familiar for this (see below). But one technique that is relatively easy to learn and very simple to use, is to use your finger to sense the amount and type of activity in the body, through the vertebrae (see p.70). Everyone can learn to dowse and this makes the diagnosis of colour energies in the spine a relatively simple activity. And once you begin to work in this way, you may find that it makes you more sensitive to working with colour in other ways, too.

Working with a pendulum

Choose a pendulum that feels comfortable to hold. Find out first which way it moves in answer to your questions. It can answer "yes", "no", or "do not know". The movement may be circular, from side to side, or forward and back. To find out, sit down, holding the pendulum so it hangs about

Using the pendulum
Once you have established how your pendulum moves for "yes", "no", and "do not know", you can use it for dowsing.

Hold the thread between your fingers, focusing your mind on your questions. Remember that these must be clear, and require only a "yes" or "no" response.

Pendulum materials
A pendulum can be made of metal, wood, or a crystal, held by a thread or a very fine chain 9-12ins (23-30cm) long. The finer the thread, the less it will resist movement.

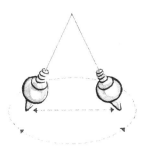

two inches (5cm) above your knees. Keep your hand with the pendulum very still. Then ask, "What is my yes?" Allow time for the pendulum to start its movement, and then remember the result. Before the pendulum stops moving, ask "what is my no?" Let the pendulum give its own direction. Do this several times daily, until you are confident about what every movement means.

Working with a pendulum is a very personal thing; always dedicate yourself to the work, and do it for the benefit of your friend or client, with no other thought or purpose. Keep your pendulum for your own use only.

Dowsing with your finger

The spine chart (see facing page) allows you to record the active energies in the human spine. All you need is a "witness", such as a lock of hair, a photograph, or a signature from your friend or client. The witness should be written on the back of the spine chart, or simply placed behind, in the case of a photograph or hair, and the chart laid on the table. It is wise to remove any written documents or printed material from any drawer underneath.

Dowsing the spine
Use the middle finger of your left hand (your right hand if you are left-handed) and start at the top of the chart (right). Let your finger hover about half an inch (1cm) above the paper. Work down the chart, vertebra by vertebra, and allow yourself to feel the sensations. You will feel nothing over the inactive vertebrae. The active ones will give you a hot, cold, repelling, or tingling sensation.

Record the result as you move down the chart, noting the strength of the response – strong, medium, or weak.

Spiritual area

The eight fused bones of the skull receive messages from our higher, spiritual self. They are not used in diagnosis because of the difficulty of interpretation.

Mental area

Colour in this area of the spine relates to the ego, thoughts, memory, and intellect.

Emotional area

These vertebrae carry information about the astral realm, or soul, your relationships, feelings such as joy, love, hate, and anger, any emotional turmoil, heartbreak, and the way we react to the world around us.

Metabolic area

These vertebrae represent issues that are connected with your physical-etheric life force, your household, routine tasks, rhythmic metabolic processes, including the digestive system, food, toxins, and drug and alcohol consumption.

Physical area

This area can provide information about your physical being, sexuality, obsessions and habits, physical ailments, survival and reproduction, exercise and sport, and other regular activities.

7 cervical vertebrae

12 thoracic vertebrae

5 lumbar vertebrae

Sacrum

Spinal diagnosis

The system of analysing colour in the spine gives yet more opportunity to diagnose the condition of the body and mind (see pp. 72-3), and another way of allowing colour into the body, for healing purposes.

Order of colours

The order of the colours within each section is the same, following the colours of the rainbow, from magenta at the top, through to red at the bottom of each section.

Colour intensity

The intensity of the colours increases toward the bottom of the spine, because this represents the physical functions, where the colours are more contracted, and therefore more dense.

The colours of health

In a balanced, healthy human being, the colours in the spine turn up repeatedly, in groups of eight, from top to bottom (see p. 71). In a healthy spine, the colour in a vertebra has a counterpart, which is its complementary colour. The original colour and its complementary are connected at an energetic level. Where the colour energies in the spine exist in complementary pairs, their energies are balanced (see p. 90). These vertebrae may also be described as "matched", or "bridged". Where the complementary colour does not appear, the original colour remains "unbridged", and represents imbalance in the body (see Chapter Five), rather like an energy still looking for somewhere else to go.

The chart below describes the significance of the colours in a healthy spine. The information makes specific reference to the four sections of the spine: the mental, emotional,

Colours in the healthy spine

MAGENTA

Mental
"Let go" or "change" You are making efforts to change and let go of old memories.

Emotional
You are letting go of old feelings, and allowing your feelings to change.

Metabolic
You are managing to leave behind domestic habits that no longer apply, and changing your eating habits where necessary.

Physical
You are making efforts to change your activities that no longer apply, and to be free of the influence of others over your lifestyle.

VIOLET

Mental
"Dignity" You are paying due respect to your personal mental activities.

Emotional
You accept and respect your own feelings as being good and dignified.

Metabolic
Your home feels like a dignified place. You are treating everything at home, including food, with respect.

Physical
You respect your body and behave in a dignified way.

BLUE

Mental
"Relaxation" Your mind is relaxed and peaceful.

Emotional
You feel peaceful and relaxed.

Metabolic
Your home life is relaxed; meals are eaten in peace.

Physical
You undertake your activities and physical work in a relaxed state.

TURQUOISE

Mental
"Immunity" You are independent and immune from other people's thoughts.

Emotional
You are coping well; other people's feelings do not impinge on you.

Metabolic
Your immune system works well; you make sufficient energy available to it.

Physical
You are behaving freely, not following the will or obligation of others.

metabolic, and physical. The colour depends on the level of activity in each vertebra (see p. 70). In reality, it would be very unlikely that all colours would show up as being active at one time. This is because daily rhythms continually alter the activities within the body (see p. 77). And as it is normal for human beings always to be in a state of progress toward a new equilibrium, some parts of the spine are likely to be more active than others at any one time. By making a series of charts, each on different days at different times, a practitioner can build up a full picture of the spinal energies and their patterns.

In practice, dowsing usually shows up activity in about half the vertebrae of the spinal column. The activity of each colour is summarized below by a word or expression that describes its characteristics.

GREEN

Mental	Emotional	Metabolic	Physical
"Balance" You have a balanced mind, and you are not letting your work affect your home life, or vice versa.	You have a balanced relationship with your partner, and you are at ease with the social structures of your life.	Your home life is stable, and you are balancing periods of activity and relaxation.	Your actions are balanced. You act at the right time.

YELLOW

Mental	Emotional	Metabolic	Physical
"Detachment" You can think clearly and make sound judgements.	You are able to detach yourself from your own and other people's feelings to see them objectively.	You can look at your home objectively, and appreciate or criticise the way you have created it.	You are able to act according to the needs of the moment.

ORANGE

Mental	Emotional	Metabolic	Physical
"Joy" Joy and happiness fill your thoughts.	Your heart is open and joyful, giving you enjoyable emotional exchanges.	Joy and pleasure at home help the digestion and give strength to the whole body.	You are able to enjoy all the physical activity that is needed of you.

RED

Mental	Emotional	Metabolic	Physical
"Strength" You have the energy to think, and to carry out all your mental requirements.	You have enough strength to be open emotionally.	Your energy for your home life means that it is in good order; so, too, is your digestive system.	You are coping well with your daily physical activities.

The body in balance

The five functions of the human body – spiritual, mental, emotional, metabolic, and physical – are always exchanging energies with each other. This never-ending movement is the best indicator of life, and while energy is being exchanged and maintained in balance, the body remains healthy. The smooth and continuous flow of energy in your body depends on your ability to acknowledge each of the five functions. This creates a unity in your being that means you can draw on all your energies in order to achieve your aims – rather like a rowing team pulling together in unison.

The idea of acknowledging all the aspects of your body's functions sounds simple, although it is probably harder for most people to carry out than you might think. If, for example, you are particularly good at producing ideas, but not so good at seeing them through, you should learn to acknowledge your physical activities more – do some gardening, for example, and get your hands dirty! This helps to "ground" you, improves your connection with the physical aspects, and will connect your mental and physical processes, enabling you to carry out your ideas. The aim is always to create a flow of energy through the emotional, mental and physical aspects of yourself. An imbalance in the flow will create problems at all levels. For example, fear can create anxious thoughts, which can lead to problems in the metabolism. You can only achieve a balanced flow by maintaining a healthy level of activity in all aspects of yourself.

The Spinal Diagnosis Chart (p. 71) is a particularly good indicator of these connections. The energetic swirl of colour in the human aura also mirrors the quality of the energy flow through the body. The colours of the aura in a healthy person have a characteristic glow and brightness (see p. 67). For example, the red energy of the base chakra (see p. 64) is bright and clear in those people whose physical and sexual lives are healthy and joyful.

Red can very easily lose its beauty in this respect when the mental and emotional energies are focused only on physical gratification. The red is then not fully imbued with the transmuted energies from the other energy centres of the body and becomes very murky. In cases of rape, the red,

Working in the garden, you will absorb the healing colour energies of nature, which vary with the changing seasons (right). An hour a day spent in a natural environment is a wonderful tonic.

sexual energy of the offender's aura is tainted with black. All centres, when not operating at their peak, including those occasions when human intentions are not "pure", become darker and unclean looking.

The active vertebrae of the spinal column are constantly maintaining an exchange of energy, and while this exchange works to produce an equilibrium, the body is in a state of health. Naturally, it is impossible to hope for a perfect state of health, because of all the external and internal changes that are going on all the time. The body is always working toward that state of perfection, rather than achieving it.

Variations in the aura

The continual flux in the energies of the aura is accentuated by normal daily activities (see right) and sleep patterns, as well as the ageing process. When you are asleep, your "container" energy (the rings of the aura) is very strong, and the activity of the chakras is less pronounced, making the ray-like energy that shines into and out of the chakras very fine in appearance. In the awake state the opposite is true. Your "content" chakra energy becomes stronger, while the surrounding layers appear finer by comparison.

Designs for movement and health

The above pattern is reproduced from a ceiling in Cleveland Hospital, England, where terminally ill cancer patients are treated. It combines the healing colours of blue and gold with a pattern that creates both movement and direction.

The pattern entices the viewer to follow its form, a representation of the head (at the top) and the rest of the body (below), with the heart in the middle. The effect of this is to encourage movement throughout the body – the anti-thesis of illness, decay, and stagnation. This movement enlivens the whole person and helps to reconnect the mind, the body, and the emotions.

During childhood and until puberty, the reds and oranges are dominant in the aura, and the time is correspondingly active and playful. By about 12 years, yellow starts to dominate, then from 24-36 years and 36-48 greens and turquoise appear more, highlighting balance and clear health, which serve family life well. The blues, violets, and magentas are more evident after 48 years of age. Blue and violet are the colours associated with teaching and serving, when we can share some of the knowledge and skills gained through life. Magenta, the dominant colour from 72 years onward, is the time for letting go – time for the next generation to take over.

Temperament and the aura

In addition to the daily changes in the natural ebb and flow of energies, and the those changes created by the ageing process, differences in temperament produce corresponding highlights in the colour energies. Rudolf Steiner distinguished the same four types of temperament that Hippocrates (c460-c377BC) first described. Sanguine types, connected

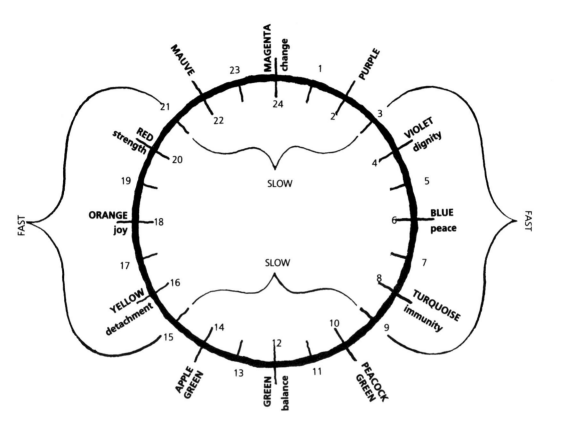

with the element air, make light of problems. They are good planners for long-term work and their aura is yellow-dominant. The melancholic pays attention to detail and is good at putting plans into practice. Prone to sadness, and sometimes "unable to see the light", the melancholic's colour is blue, connected with the element of water.

The choleric type, associated with the element of fire, sometimes acts impatiently, and often before thinking. Red is the dominant colour. Patience characterizes the phlegmatic – connected with the earth element and the colour green. The phlegmatic person waits for things to happen, on the basis that "the mountain will come to Mohammed".

Daily rhythms in the body

The rhythms of the day and night affect the energy flow in your body, producing changing levels of activity. The daily cycle of 24 hours is divided into intervals of two hours. Each of these highlights a style of activity that is associated with a particular organ, and corresponds to a colour. A further pattern is superimposed on this two-hourly rhythm: the hours between 9pm and 3am represent a general slowing of energy. Between 3am and 9am energy levels increase, then ebb again until 3pm. After this, the activity of early evening begins.

CHAPTER FIVE

feeling off colour

As you progress through life, you will inevitably experience phases of good health and bad health. Your physical, mental, emotional, and spiritual development is the product of your genetic patterning and your life experience, including the food you eat and the quality of the environmental input. Even your thoughts affect the way you feel. This delicate balance of possibilities means that sometimes you may undermine your health very easily; at other times you will be well equipped to deal with life's changes.

Colour therapy tests and diagnostic techniques are all based on the belief that illness is predictable from personality analysis. The thought processes are the origin of all disease, which may then become manifest in the emotions and the physical body (see facing page). Mental and emotional developments cause changes in your colour energies, so these are reliable indicators of illness that could become evident at a later date. Specific changes in the aura, or in the colour energies of the spine, relate to specific problems that may exist. Because of this, colour treatment can detect and work on these problems before the illness manifests in the body. This approach differs from Western medicine, which can only begin to treat symptoms that have already penetrated into the physical body.

Illness and its diagnosis

This chapter looks first at the significance of illness and then at its diagnosis through colour. It puts illness into a context; the product both of physical changes sometimes connected with bacteria, viruses, and other agents of disease, and of mental and emotional imbalances that arise throughout the normal course of life.

Colour therapy uses a variety of techniques for diagnosis, some of which you can learn with little training. All of them are described in this chapter, and some can be mastered from the information given; others need additional training. Colour practitioners may be trained in some or all of them. Some practitioners work on aura perception, using changes in the shape and colour of an aura to give information on a condition (see pp. 86-9). Others dowse to detect the quality of colour energies in the spine, then analyse the balance of these energies by means of a chart, where all the information

Transforming your negative thoughts

If you are entertaining negative thoughts, or clinging on to negative attitudes, confront them, and you will be in a better position to let them go. If these thoughts go unrecognized, they tend to turn up in the emotional area as bad feelings, and much more deeply anchored than before.
Relax, let go of all your tensions throughout your body. Breathe normally, then surround yourself in the colour magenta, which allows you to let go of your thoughts. By letting go of this negativity, you emerge strengthened, and ready for the next step in your personal development.

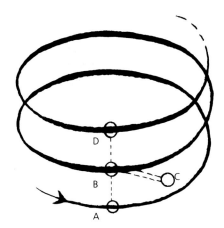

The development of illness
Your journey through life can be illustrated as a spiral. Where there has been a change in your mental state (point A, left), when you again find yourself in a similar situation (on the next turn of the spiral, point B) you will encounter that change at an emotional level. If your emotional response is resolved, you shift into a new pattern of life and continue on a slightly altered spiral path (point C). If your emotions are left unresolved you will meet them again in the future, but this time at a metabolic level (point D). Once the problem manifests in your metabolic processes, your life force is weakened; the road back to health will be a longer one.

is recorded (see pp. 90-2). Psychological tests (pp. 94-7) can supply additional information on your personality and needs. In using these tests, you have strong indicators of your health tendencies.

The Colour Reflection Reading (pp. 94-5) monitors the way your personality and life events are affecting your health, and directs you in the use of therapeutic colour techniques. The Lüscher colour test (p. 96) also produces a detailed personality analysis. Art therapy (pp. 96-7) looks at the interaction between personality and health by analysing paintings. Each section includes a discussion of the individual use and value of these diagnostic tools.

Health and movement in the body
Your body is in a continual state of flux. Changes occur at every level within you and your health is intimately connected with your ability to accept these changes. Movement of every kind is natural in a healthy being. Without movement, development would not take place.

If the movement in your body – from the beat of your heart, to cellular activity – becomes sluggish, your body will cease to function efficiently and you may become ill. If this happens, accept the illness as a challenge, as an opportunity to "move on", both mentally and physically. By doing this, you progress toward a more healthy body and a more highly developed mind. Illness is a learning process, a lesson on the way to greater consciousness.

The ideal state
Your body and mind have a "memory" of the ideal state, deep seated in your subconscious, but also available to your super-conscious, or higher conscious self. By getting in touch with these parts of your mind, for example by the methods of relaxed visualization described on page 52, you can begin to find the pattern of your personal needs. By looking into yourself, you can begin the process of healing.

The challenge of illness

Pain, or a diagnosed disease, is bound to make you start thinking about how you can regain your health. Doctors can provide doses of sophisticated drugs, all of which affect your physiology, sometimes altering your moods as well. They may make the symptoms go away, but frequently bring with them their own side effects and only provide a temporary respite from the disease symptoms. Real cures demand the patient to take part in the healing process, otherwise the treatment is merely a "cover up" for a cure.

By looking into yourself to understand your illnesss, you may isolate habits connected with your diet, your sleep, or your physical environment, that prevent you from functioning at your best. You may, equally, examine your thoughts and feelings – for these are at the root of all chemical changes in your body. Negative attitudes such as guilt, hatred, revenge, not being able to forgive, and holding grudges, affect not only mental activity but are soon reflected in your emotions and your physical body. Just by taking these first steps, you will put yourself in a closer relationship with your body and mind, and you may be able to address thoughts and behaviours that were upsetting the healthy flow of your body's energy.

Understanding yourself

The path to health is different for everybody. People with apparently the same illness may nonetheless experience different symptoms, while people with the same symptoms may need to follow a different path to health.

Energy in, energy out

Your ability to keep energy moving within you depends not only on the free passage of energy in your body that unites your mental, emotional, and physical aspects, but also on taking energy in and letting it go. Think of your body as continually breathing – not only the breath that fills your lungs, but a pulsing energy always flowing in and flowing out. Your health and personal development depend just as much on this continual exchange of energy in and out of your body, as on the free circulation of energy inside you. Ultimately, the result of all movement ceasing is death – no movement into or out of the body.

Children's development

Children up to the age of puberty are accumulating energy from the instream. After puberty, they have a strong enough sense of self to give, in the sense of being generous with their own spirit. Expecting predictable standards of behaviour from children before this age, for example by trying to "show off" a child's particular ability on request, damages a child's need to reveal him or herself at the appropriate time. This behaviour also exhausts children's energies, thus robbing them of the strength they need to build up inside.

Cosmic etheric energy

The energy that you take in originates from cosmic energy. This is the life force that underlies your ability to breathe, eat, grow, have feelings, and think.

The physical energy from food and drink is just part of the energy that sustains us in life. Both cosmic and physical energies are types of etheric, or "life-supporting" energies. While food provides the physical, or metabolic etheric energy, life itself depends on cosmic etheric energy.

Instream

The intake of cosmic etheric energy depends partly on your genetic tendencies: you are born with a capacity to welcome the outside world or to turn your back on it. Your experiences as a child and adolescent also have a strong influence on this instream of energy. If you as an individual have been fully accepted for what you are, then you will be open to the cosmic, life-giving energies that surround you. Cosmic energy streams in to happy people more than it does to those who are sad. In denying themselves their own happiness, sad people also deny themselves the strength and vitality that could support and replenish them.

Outstream

The outstream of energy depends on how well your own expressions of energy are met by others. If others try to curb these energies in you, then you may suffer from depression and frustration. The free flow of your energy includes the ability to express yourself freely, and not to be constantly undermined.

Working with a counsellor

Whatever type of colour therapy you go for, the first stage is to talk to the practitioner in order to build up a picture of your personality and needs. The particular questions depend on the individual situation – the reasons for you starting treatment in the first place, and the skills and experience that the practitioner brings to the therapy session.

The two main questions that the practitioner will ask in your introductory counselling session are, firstly, how your behaviour (or your condition, if you have a specific ailment) and feelings change throughout the day. When are you particularly active? When do you feel particularly tired or sluggish? This question helps give the practitioner some insight into the colour energies that are working well – where the colours in your aura would be pure and bright – and those that might need attention during the therapy sessions.

The second question is about your favourite and most disliked colours. Following this, the counsellor tries to find the origins of these likes and dislikes, by asking questions about situations that might have given rise to the good and bad associations. The reason for trying to identify these good and bad psychological associations is that both can create an imbalance in your day to day colour exposure. You may well avoid a much needed colour, just because of an unpleasant past association. The aim is to regain an equal acceptance of all colours.

A third question might arise, about your favourite pastimes. The answer to this tells the counsellor how wide the gap is between how you spend your time and how you would like to spend it.

The counsellor may go on to discuss various aspects of your life, corresponding to the four sections of the spine (see p. 71). These questions are not always easy to answer; they need thought and insight into aspects of your life that you may not have previously considered. The key question is "How well do you acknowledge the mental, emotional, metabolic, and physical areas of your life?" Your answers not only help the practitioner to interpret your spine chart (see p. 91). They will also enable you to see for yourself whether you accept or reject your life at any of those levels.

For example, in the metabolic region of your spine, the relevant issues surround your home life, the regularity with which you conduct your domestic arrangements, and the amount of care you put into them (see p. 71). If you acknowledge the importance of these issues, it will mean that the energy in that area of your spine should be pure and bright, and the colours that appear in that area are likely to be balanced, or "bridged" (see p. 72). If you do not acknowledge the need to give the metabolic area of your life this sort of attention, then you are likely to be blocking the energies in that area, and this may create discolourations. The blocked energies prevent the smooth and free flow of energy throughout your whole body; your mental, emotional, metabolic, and physical areas are no longer well connected and the balance goes out of your life. Eventually, illness may result. By diagnosing this sort of problem before the onset of any illness, you can receive appropriate advice concerning your domestic life, and put right the problem before it even becomes apparent. Your answers also tell the practitioner how ready you are to make changes in your life.

Underlying all this is the need for you as patient to want to co-operate with your counsellor. Counselling can help to elicit information that you may want to share, but that you find difficult to articulate. But no professional counsellor will make you give information before you feel ready.

Case study

David suffered from severe migraine, and the colour blue came up repeatedly from the Spinal Diagnosis. Light treatment with the colour blue was unsuccessful, and he resisted using blue visualizations. For some reason he was unable to respond to the colour.

By the fourth treatment, the only solution seemed to be to talk to David about his past, and to see if blue had an emotional attachment that was blocking the treatment. David told me that he never wore blue clothes, nor decorated his home with blue; he was uncomfortable with the colour. I asked him if he had been frightened or upset at any time when the colour blue was present. He recalled a train crash in which he was involved when he was eight years old. The train was de-railed. It was night time and he fell out of his bunk. Above the door of the compartment was a small, blue nightlight.

Having recognized the root of David's problem with the colour blue, I encouraged him to try to overcome it, and suggested that, by accepting the colour again, he might well find relief from his migraines. It represented an energy in him that he was not acknowledging. After practising by relaxing into the colour blue, subsequent treatments were more successful. David was able to accept its healing powers. A few months later, he chose to redecorate his office in shades of blue. He reported that his migraines had all but ceased.

Diet and your aura

Even the food you eat has an impact on the quality of colours in your aura. Highly processed foods, and especially those that are packaged, sealed, and stored, lack energy and produce a correspondingly thin aura. If you eat too much meat, your aura becomes denser. If you have a very faint aura a practitioner may advise you to eat more fish or meat.

Changes in the aura

Your aura fluctuates, as already said, as a response to changes both within you and in the environment. The two main fluctuations are in the colour and the shape. Most of the colour changes result from changes within, and signal a slowing, a speeding, or a blocking of energy in the body. The changes in shape are usually inflicted from outside. The size of the aura may also change in both cases, contracting or expanding, depending on how free you feel to behave naturally, or whether you are being constrained. Many of the small changes rectify themselves through your own natural adjustments. More severe changes can be dealt with by using colour breathing and visualization; treatment with coloured light may be needed for more problematic alterations in the aura.

Colour changes

The rainbow colours of your aura breathe, expanding and contracting, so that all the colours start to dance. In health, the colours are pure, bright, and quite dense, or strong. Happiness creates sparkling movement, and a slightly shiny effect. Feelings of love overlay the aura with the colours of amethyst and rose quartz. Sadness represents a low energy state, and the colours become slightly dimmer, even dull. Dreamy people also have faint auras; they are less grounded physically, so the colours are correspondingly less solid.

The two most common discolourations of the aura are brown and grey. They are the results of "energy in" not equalling "energy out" (see p. 82). A grey discolouration suggests you are creating a barrier to an energy input of some description. This could be at the mental, emotional, metabolic, or physical level. At the mental level, it might be an unwillingness to take on somebody's ideas; at the emotional level, fear of an emotional involvement; at the metabolic level, a lack of desire for food.

The position of the discolouration in the aura corresponds to the level of the problem. Problems at the mental level are seen in the outer layers; emotional, metabolic, and physical problems come progressively closer to the body. The discolouration also relates to the position of the fine, ray-like energy of the chakras (see pp. 64-5). For example, fear of an

A child has a naturally shiny, luminous aura (right), with red as the strongest colour, reflecting the natural activity and playfulness of childhood (see p. 76).

**Using discolourations
for diagnosis**
*The chart below lists the significance
of energy blockages in the aura.
These are represented by brown
discolourations (holding on to energy)
and discolourations of grey (blocking
energy input).*

emotional involvement will show as grey in the green layer
(which is connected to the heart) and also grey in the area of
the heart chakra.

Brown signifies "holding on" to energy that needs to be
let go. Even having a cold discolours the aura in this way,
and represents a negative attitude, such as "Even if this is
bad, I shall hold on to it". Someone who freely takes, but
rarely gives, is more likely to have this brown discolouration
of congested energies.

Chakra/Spinal area	BROWN (holding on to energies)	GREY (blocking energy input)	Treatment Colour
CROWN/MENTAL	Obsessional thinking		MAGENTA
		Thoughtlessness	YELLOW
PITUITARY/MENTAL	Obsessional images		DEEP BLUE
		Lack of images	ORANGE
THROAT/MENTAl	Too talkative		VIOLET
		Silence/autism/ perfectionism	YELLOW
THYMUS/EMOTIONAL	Mean		ORANGE
		Overgenerous/not able to receive	BLUE
HEART/EMOTIONAL	Closed/unresponsive		TURQUOISE
		Too open/indiscriminate	RED
SOLAR PLEXUS/EMOTIONAL	Fear		BLUE
		Overconfidence	GREEN
SACRAL/METABOLIC	Weak sex drive		RED
		Strong sex drive	BLUE
BASE/PHYSICAL	Lethargy		RED
		Overactivity	GREEN

Shape changes

The most likely cause of shape changes to the aura is shock.
A shock may make your aura shift away from your head; it
may also move away from your heart, leaving both head
and heart unprotected. The effect of this is to separate your
spirit self from your physical sensations. If the shock is severe

enough to shift your aura away from your heart region, your emotions will no longer feel connected with your body. You might feel as though you are about to faint, or even as though you are on the verge of a nervous breakdown.

A shock that is not quite so severe, such as witnessing a bad car accident, may regularize after about 24 hours. During that time you feel vulnerable, insecure, and unable to accept any form of responsibility. You lack connection between your personality and your own mental activities.

A mild shock, such as cutting yourself, or falling down a few steps, may shift your aura briefly away from your head. Taking a deep breath is usually enough to bring your protective aura back into place. You should also try visualizing the colour blue, and using your colour breathing techniques (see p. 54), breathing blue in, and orange out. End with a green visualization to regain a feeling of balance.

Electro-convulsive therapy can also move the aura away from the body. The etheric sheath maintains the life systems of the body. Colour treatment can help re-unite the chakra energies and their bodily counterparts, and reconnect the soul and spirit to the physical and life forces.

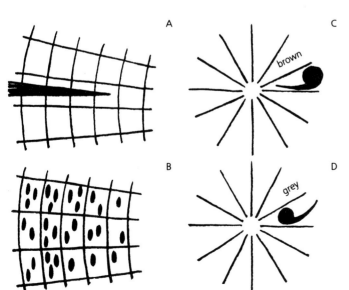

Unhealthy patterns in the aura
The use of hard drugs can create wedge-shaped areas in the aura that have no colour, and therefore appear black (see diagram A and p. 90). This indicates a serious depletion of the body's energy.

Flecks or shadows in the aura (diagram B) are usually a reaction to more minor toxins, such as alcohol or nicotine. If no more toxins are ingested these flecks will disperse within about 4 hours. However, if the intake increases the shadows in the aura will increase.

Brown discolouration of the aura (diagram C) results from an inability to let go of energies (see facing page). Conversely, a grey area (diagam D) indicates a barrier to accepting energies (see p. 86).

Negative emotions can also alter the shape of your aura, although not on the scale of the shock reaction. Hate and jealousy produce a jagged edge to the auric layers, which weakens the structure and effectively means that your protection is undermined.

Hard drugs also give the aura a similar jagged edge, which becomes irreparable if bad drug habits continue. Like a log of wood that dries out, the aura can begin to "split", making wedge-like areas of depletion. These are colourless intrusions into the aura that can, over a period of time, reach the centre, leading to complete exhaustion. The wedges affect the chakra energy, and may deplete any of the glands. The colours in the aura that surround the body become cloudy.

Sensations
As you dowse, you may feel sensations of heat, cold, tingling, or repulsion. Tingling is a good sign of vibrant health, while heat, cold, or repulsion suggest that your energy is out of balance. An experienced practitioner takes this into account when making a spine chart.

Colour changes in the spine

Dowsing the spine can give you a very clear indication of the colour energies in the body. By dowsing with the middle finger, as explained in Chapter Four, and feeling the reactions, you can then record the information on a spinal diagnosis chart (see opposite page) in order to create a clear picture of health.

As you work down the vertebrae on the spine chart on page 70, your finger registers responses of different strengths, indicating which of the vertebrae are currently active. Record the strength of the sensation on your spinal diagnosis chart (see below and opposite page).

Key to response strength

very weak	−	−
weak		−
weak to medium	−	0
medium		0
medium to strong	0	+
strong		+
very strong	+	+

Typically, about 16 out of the 32 spinal vertebrae are active, sometimes as many as 18, rarely fewer than 11. If your dowsing finds more than 18 active vertebrae, it may be that you need more practice to distinguish sensation from non-sensation. However, some people who are exhausting themselves may show up more than 18 active vertebrae.

Spinal diagnosis chart

Working on the spine chart

Colour the active vertebrae on the spine chart, using the colours indicated by the vertebrae. The rainbow pattern of eight colours is repeated in each section of the spine.

Mark on one side of the chart the strength of the response.

In order to locate the comple-mentary colours with ease, it is useful to draw the complementary colour of each active vertebra in a column by the side. Then, starting with the uppermost active (coloured) vertebra, look for that same colour in the column, starting at the bottom. Your aim is to join the complementary colour as far down the spine as possible. Then take the next coloured vertebra down and do the same thing. Repeat this, always choosing the complementary farthest away, until you have joined, or "bridged", all the complementary colours. You are then left with colours that are active, but unbridged. These indicate colours for treatment (see Chapter Six).

Refer back to the chart to see which of these colours gave the strongest signal. That is the colour for treatment. Date the chart.

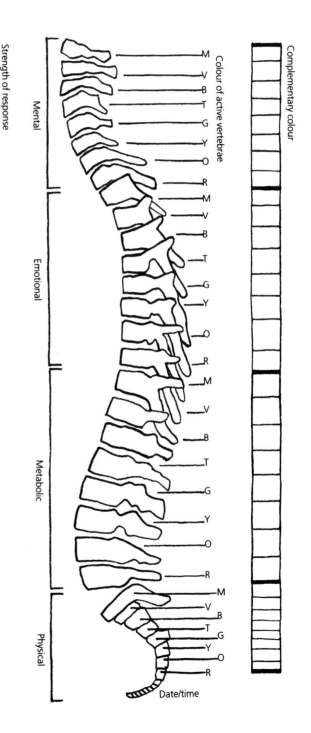

The chart produces a unique pattern for each individual. Because of the energy changes in the body during the day (see p. 77), you should record the time of the test. Make a new spinal diagnosis before any treatment, in order to record the changes over time.

Once you have filled in a spinal diagnosis chart and joined the pairs of complementary colours (see p. 91), you can begin to look at what the colours mean. You might have several pairs of bridged colours, and several unbridged colours. If all the colours are bridged, it suggests a healthy exchange of energy within the body. The links between the mental, emotional, metabolic, and physical aspects of the body represent an acknowledgement of those functions and a free flow of communication between them. A link between the mental and physical areas is particularly good because the connection from top to bottom works also through the emotional and metabolic layers. Unbridged colours suggest the treatment colours; use the one that gave the strongest signal (see Chapter Six).

Using the information from the spine chart, you can transfer the details on to a simple résumé, which will help you see how well the energetic connections are working. The résumé allows you to summarize several spine charts, and show you the changes over time, or the progress of every treatment session. You can also use your summary of a series of spine charts to show up the underlying personality characteristics.

Using the spinal diagnosis chart

Mark the bridged pairs as shown (right). This highlights how many sections are involved in the connection. Mark the unbridged colours in their colour, or in a symbol or short form for the colour (as right).

Unbridged colours indicate a lack of that colour in that section of the body and need treatment. If there is more than one unbridged colour, enhance the unbridged colour that has the strongest signal (for example, mark it with a cross). This is the colour to use in treatment.

The number of columns used for the summary of each spine chart will depend on how many vertebrae are active, and how many of these are bridged. Remember to mark the date and time of the spinal diagnosis.

Mark the bridged pairs and then the unbridged colours start with the uppermost active vertebra and its pair.

Summary chart of the spinal diagnosis

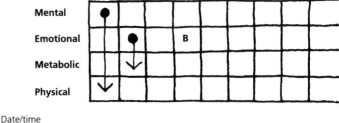

Date/time

Key

Bridged colours

Unbridged colour   B   (see key on p. 91)

Analysis

The ideal connection is between complementary pairs in the mental and physical regions of the spine. Some colour pairs may be bridged within a single section. This indicates a healthy acknowledgement of the activities of that section, but a less free flow of energies overall.

Once you have completed the summary chart, look back at the strength and type of signal you received from the unbridged colours while dowsing. If you have found more than one unbridged colour, use as the treatment colour the one that produced the strongest signal.

Refer back to the descriptions on page 71 to see how each section functions. With practice it becomes straightforward to analyse the connections between these different sections. The following case studies show how to build a picture from the spine chart.

The meanings of the unbridged colours

Mental	Emotional	Metabolic	Physical
Magenta You are not letting go or changing your old thoughts.	**Magenta** You are not letting go of old feelings.	**Magenta** You are ignoring your changing needs in food and household.	**Magenta** You need to change your daily or weekly plan of actions.
Violet You have no respect or dignity for your own mental work.	**Violet** You lack dignity, and are ashamed of your feelings.	**Violet** You are treating your home and belongings with disrespect.	**Violet** Your body feels undignified.
Blue Your mental process is not relaxed; you lack peace.	**Blue** You are not relaxing, and cannot enjoy your emotions.	**Blue** You take no time to eat, to study, or to enjoy your home.	**Blue** You are not giving yourself enough time to do things peacefully.
Turquoise You have no immunity from other people's thoughts.	**Turquoise** You are unable to be immune from the feelings of others.	**Turquoise** You have a digestive weakness, or inflammatory condition.	**Turquoise** You are too easily influenced by those around you.
Green Your mental process lacks balance.	**Green** Problems in personal relationships may be causing you upset.	**Green** Your home life lacks balance: the same might apply to your diet.	**Green** You are doing things without order or plan.
Yellow You lack objectivity because you do not detach yourself.	**Yellow** You cannot detach from other people's emotions.	**Yellow** Look after your calcium metabolism; you may have an arthritic condition.	**Yellow** You are doing things which are now no longer necessary.
Orange You experience no joy or happiness doing mental work.	**Orange** You lack joy and happiness.	**Orange** This may be an indicator of anorexia.	**Orange** You experience no happiness or joy in your activities.
Red You have no energy or strength, and are easily tired.	**Red** You have no strength or energy for expressing your feelings.	**Red** You lack energy because of bad digestion.	**Red** You lack sufficient physical strength or energy.

Personality assessment

Personality assessments help give you insight into your patterns of behaviour. This may, in turn, suggest how your health might be affected, and how you might benefit by working with colour, once you have this knowledge.

Colour Reflection Reading

This technique is a practical way of working with the psychology of colour and produces straightforward colour advice. It was devised in 1985 by Dorothy and Howard Sun and is presented in a shortened form here to show how the technique works. Refer to Living Colour in the Resources section (p. 124) for more details. Colour Reflection Readings take about one hour and require the interpretation of a colour counsellor. Other colour diagnoses and treatments use the range of techniques described in Chapters Five and Six.

Eight colours are presented in shapes (see p. 47) printed on white card, in two rows. By making three colour choices, you can access your innermost thoughts and feelings directly. The Colour Reflection Reading uses colour as a new language to reflect information related to our physical, emotional, and mental wellbeing.

Analysis

The first colour represents your true essence, your basic personality. The second colour relates to your present condition at a physical, emotional, mental, and spiritual level. It reflects your deep, subconscious needs, and your main challenges. The third colour indicates how you might take your next step, to a new level of personal awareness.

The exercise

Choose the three colours that you prefer at this moment. Do not think about it; let your intuitive mind do the work, and choose your colours straight away, rather than allowing your judgements to interfere. Forget about your "favourite" colours and any associations that sway your feelings. Place the three chosen colours separately in front of you in order of preference.

The significance of your colour choices

First position
You are an initiator, a pioneer, a creator. Active and physical. You need to harmonize your emotions with your logic to obtain the equilibrium you seek.

Second position
Your challenge is to energize yourself, but without exhausting your resources. You need to reduce domination and work on expressing your warmth and friendship.

Third position
You want to feel active, but you are exhausted. Try to replenish yourself and quieten your system.

First position
Joyful and ebullient. Sometimes tired through over-activity. Listen to yourself, learn to be still, and trust your basic instinctive nature.

Second position
Your greatest challenge is to make time for yourself, and find stillness in body and mind.

Third position
You may have inwardly withdrawn. You can be more courageous and confident. Try to be willing to take more risks than usual.

First position
You tend to search constantly for information. Good with words, You can be dominating. Your work probably carries responsibility.

Second position
The challenge is to think about your physical self, not just your mental ability, so that you can express the energy relevant to now.

Third position
You need to work out how to expand your mind, perhaps through education, to bring optimism into your life. A holiday in the sun could help.

First position
A personality full of balance, sometimes lacking in spontaneity through over-caution. Neat and efficient, with an affinity for natural materials.

Second position
Your main challenge is to express your emotions, and to come to terms with emotional hurts. You may be acting out of unfulfilled need.

Third position
By making more contact with people, you will lift your spirits, and feel more valuable, less serious. Guilt and inertia will also diminish.

First position
You are imaginative and full of fresh ideas. You make yourself clear, you are popular, and can deal with demanding situations. You have insight and are spiritually orientated.

Second position
Learn to control the demands of others and give yourself time to reflect. You may need to cleanse your body, mind, and emotions to prevent toxification and illness.

Third position
You welcome the challenge of change as part of a personal transformation, although this can produce fear, turmoil, and upset.

First position
Gentle by nature, you are also reliable. You make people feel secure. You value truth and honesty; at times your inward searching is too self-absorbed, making you isolated.

Second position
Your strength is your silence and knowingness; your challenge is to express yourself more directly, in order to avoid inertia and melancholy.

Third position
Be flexible enough to take a more earthly, practical attitude toward daily life. Use relaxation to restore yourself, but not as a *modus operandi* or means of escape.

First position
A mixture of red and blue, you apply your spirituality in a grounded way. Aesthetic, artistic, and with a sense of ceremony, you do not always feel sure that you will achieve your vision.

Second position
Although you are likely to be in a position of authority, your challenge is to ask for acknowledgement. Otherwise you may become negative about responsibility. Persevere.

Third position
Violet encourages you to use your creativity, and to share it with others. Practise using your innate capacity for faith, intuition, and wisdom.

First position
Kind, co-operative, and friendly. Often very mature, with a deep understanding of life. Likely to be working in the caring professions.

Second position
Your challenge is to balance giving and receiving because you tend to neglect your own needs. Learn to receive as well. Nurture yourself; respect your own needs.

Third position
As you strive to blend the basic life forces (red) with heavenly power (violet), you risk developing a grandiose self-image. Let go, and allow the gentle part of your nature to shine.

Case study

Harry is 29 years old, of average build and about 5'10″ (1.78m) tall. He is a computer operator; intelligent with a quiet disposition. He wore a faded **brown** shirt with **navy blue** trousers. When Harry made his colour choices, **blue** was his first choice, **green** his second, and **orange** his third.

First position – BLUE

This colour speaks of a quiet, gentle, and peaceful individual, someone whose tendency is to be self absorbed and introspective. **"Blue** *people", like Harry, value qualities such as truth and honesty and believe in approaching life carefully and without brashness. They have a keen eye for beautiful things but are not overly materialistic. Harry agreed that these attributes were true of his personality.*

Harry seemed to lack in confidence and as a result appeared dull and non-expressive. His bland facial expressions and monotonous tone of voice revealed his lack of aliveness and a deep-rooted sadness. When we brought this to Harry's attention he expressed that he often experienced bouts of depression. All of the above are fairly common traits for **blue** *personality types.*

Harry was uninterested in job promotions and even in spending time out with friends. Most of his evenings he spent at home on his own. Harry's challenge was to get on with life in a positive way instead of becoming submerged in a melancholic state.

Second position – GREEN

Green *in the second position reflected Harry's wish to get out into wide open spaces. He loved the wild countryside and said that whenever he sat on top of a mountain, cliff, or hill-top, he experienced a deep state of freedom. It was clear that Harry gained tremendous pleasure and inner fulfilment from such introspective experiences. Then he expressed how much he wished he could spend more time outside. We suggested that he may be feeling trapped subconsciously, which he acknowledged. He wished he could leave his job as a computer operator. "Being cooped up in a stuffy office all day" was not his idea of how he wanted to spend the rest of his life. Harry wanted to use his creativity and express himself in a more meaningful way that would give him more inner satisfaction.*

Third position – ORANGE

This colour suggests that Harry should take a risk and go beyond his normal way of operating. By careful planning and taking constructive steps of action, Harry could begin the process of making moves toward fulfilling his innermost desires. **Orange** *complements the* **blue** *in the first position. This means that his goals are in alignment with his true nature/ essence. This will help empower Harry to fulfill his true potential, bringing him joy and happiness and helping him to regain the inner spark and zest for life. We would recommend* **orange** *for Harry as the colour most suited to his long-term needs, while he would require* **green** *colour energy most whenever he felt trapped and caged in.*

Action and advice

Before Harry could experience the energy of the colour **orange** and use it productively, he needed to work with the **green** colour energy for a while. We suggested that he should attend some Colour Counselling sessions to help become more objective about his personal situation and help him achieve his goals and create what he really wanted in his life. Through his changing choices in the Colour Reflection Reading in these sessions we could monitor his progress.

Harry really needed to work with his main challenge, reflected in his second position with the colour **green.** Colour Counselling sessions would help speed up the transition between **green** and **orange,** which would assist him to take whatever steps he felt were necessary to make real his aspirations in life. To date, Harry has received eight sessions over a four-month period. He no longer sees his situation at work as dull and dreary, but as a means to support him in his transition. His goal is stronger than ever and within the last four months he has been to the countryside hiking almost every second weekend. Harry is a much happier person and has begun to realize his own potential for creating his own reality.

The Lüscher Test

The Lüscher colour test is based on presenting a series of coloured cards to a patient. Devised by Dr Max Lüscher, it has been used by psychologists and physicians since 1947. In the shortened version of the test, the practitioner asks you as the patient to place eight colours in order of preference. Your choices provide information about both your conscious and unconscious mind, your areas of stress, imbalances in your glandular system, and other physiological information. A trained practitioner can diagnose illness and, in some cases, forecast the outcome of an illness.

The basic colours of the test are the four "psychological primaries": blue, yellow, red, and green. The interpretation of the colour choices is derived from the immediate physiological response, which is closely associated to deeper needs. Blue engenders calmness, while yellow (nearest to the colour of natural light) brings activity. The brightness of yellow breaks down chemicals at the back of the eye – catabolism – while the darkness of blue allows rebuilding – anabolism. The same contrast is true of red and green; red breaks down and green rebuilds.

Your choice of a particular colour depends on the extent to which your body needs anabolism or catabolism. If, for example, you are psychically or physically in need of emotional peace, physical regeneration, and release from tension or stress, then the instinctive response will be to choose darker colours. If you need to dissipate energy by mental or physical activity, your instinctive response will be toward brighter colours. In this way, the colours produce a sophisticated reading of your personality and needs.

Experienced colour practitioners may feel ill at ease with the Lüscher Test. Colour therapy takes into account the impact of the shape and form of the colour being applied (see pp. 46-7). If you react in one way to the playing card shapes of the Lüscher Test, you could well react in a different way if they were all triangles, or diamond–shaped, for example. Some experimental tests confirm this.

The Lüscher Test is nonetheless a useful tool for investigating personality characteristics, though its healing application is limited.

Colours and their meaning

The significance of the eight colours in the shortened Lüscher Test depends on where they are placed in the scale of preference. When placed in the first, or "most preferred" position, their meanings closely resemble the meaning that colour practitioners attach to them, as follows

Grey *Borderline, neutral, lack of commitment.*

Blue *Peace, tranquillity, calm.*

Green *Persistence, constancy, resistance to change.*

Red *Action, effectiveness, the "impact of the will".*

Yellow *Spontaneous enjoyment of action, uninhibited expansiveness, relaxation, release from burdens.*

Violet *Union of red and blue, wish fulfilment, intuitive understanding, sometimes irresponsibility, emotional immaturity.*

Brown *Contains red, but without red's vitality, strong sensation of bodily senses.*

Black *Extinction, negation.*

healing with colour

Once you are familiar with the diagnostic methods described in Chapter Five, you can consult the chart on the facing page to see what forms of treatment to use. This chapter demonstrates and describes the tools and techniques of colour therapy. It describes how a practitioner starts the healing process (see below), then presents the methods for colour treatments. These fall into two main categories: those that use pigment colour (see pp. 102-6) and those that use coloured light (see pp. 108-22).

In the first category, using the colour consciousness exercise (see pp. 103-6) helps to stimulate your memory, and your creative thinking. It can also help to heal paralysis following a stroke, and improve the nervous system, and eyesight. Using coloured silks, clothes, and foods (see p. 105) gives you ways to back up a practitioner's treatments between sessions.

Coloured light represents the most subtle, and therefore the most powerful, way to use colour in healing. The most important development in colour therapy has been the use of coloured light equipment (see pp. 110-13), but there are other ways to harness the power of colour. Colour breathing and visualization techniques were described in Chapter Three; this chapter describes accessories to light treatments, from the colour bath (see p. 114) that delivers coloured light refracted through water, to the eye healing lamp (see p. 116), and the healing qualities of coloured oils (see p. 117), and crystals (see pp. 117-18). The chapter also discusses how to combine methods of treatment, and how and when to bring treatment to a close (see p. 122). You can carry out most of the treatments for yourself at home, although the coloured light treatments on pages 110-13 should only be carried out by a specialist colour practitioner (see p. 111).

Receiving a patient

When a practitioner greets a patient, the first sensation on meeting comes from the emotions – the heart area, otherwise described as the soul. When you greet another person, you may not be aware of this level of the encounter; you probably allow your intellect to step in and make a mental appraisal of the person and the situation. Such an immediate appraisal often overrides the original intuitive experience of your own soul. The mental appraisal, which always follows the heart reaction, may justify your original feeling, but equally it might distort it by making an intellectual judgement that goes against your intuition. Trusting your immediate emotional response makes an important start to the healing process. It allows you to remain open to the messages that a person is giving you. The third part of your immediate experience is simply that of being confronted by another physical being (see pp. 44-5).

AILMENTS	COLOURED CLOTHES	COLOURED SILKS	SOLARIZED WATER	FOOD	COLOUR BREATHING	COLOUR VISUALIZATION	EYE STRENGTHENING CHARTS	COLOUR CONSCIOUSNESS	COLOURED LIGHTS
Migraine						●			●
Asthma									●
Eczema	●	●		●					●
Insomnia			●		●			●	
Obsessive thoughts						●			
Memory loss								●	
Depression		●				●			●
Digestive disorders		●		●					
Lethargy	●								●
Short/long sight							●		
Colds			●	●					●
Inflammations	●	●							●
High blood pressure	●	●				●			●
Low blood pressure	●	●				●			●
*Angina pectoris	●					●			●
Arthritis/rheumatism				●	●	●			●
*Cancer	●								●
*AIDS	●								●

*not to be treated without medical supervision

Underlying these three "confrontations" is the practitioner's meeting with the patient as a spiritual being manifest as a physical person. By acknowledging a patient at a spiritual level, and doing this first and foremost through the heart, and by trusting these feelings, the practitioner fully accepts the patient, and this is the first step toward treatment.

Spirituality and healing

Colour therapy works on freeing the energy flow of the body. Fundamental to the healing process is the link between every person and a higher consciousness. This consciousness may be expressed as a universal power, God, or as a "oneness of being". The link can be called your "spirituality". The healing process requires the physical, emotional, and mental functions to work smoothly and in unison so that the energy of your body interchanges freely with the energy of the universe.

The practitioner, in the role of counsellor, talks to the patient (see pp. 84–5), and from this builds a picture of the most appropriate forms of treatment (see chart p. 101). The treatment may continue for several months, or be complete in one consultation (see p. 122). The practitioner may use a combination of several techniques, including giving the patient colour exercises to do at home, in order to maintain the progress between treatment sessions with the practitioner.

Colour consciousness exercise

This exercise presents colour and shape in combination, thus engaging both the creative, right side and the logical, left side of the brain (see p. 46). The colours and forms are presented with their complementaries (see left). The first shape is the "container" and the second its "content" (see p. 47). These polarized energies increase your response to the image dramatically. The final card combines the two colours and shapes. Working toward integrating these challenges you on a mental, emotional, and physical level.

The exercise will improve your memory, your ingenuity, and your inventiveness. It also encourages creativity and artistic growth in children. As a healing technique, you can use the exercise to help insomnia, improve the nervous system, exercise the eyesight, and help in cases of paralysis after a stroke.

The exercise

To use the shapes, redraw the solid colour to approximately 4.5ins (11cms) square, using paint or felt-tip pens. Place the first set of three cards on a wall 4-5 feet (1.2-1.5m) away from you. Fix your eyes on the first (container) shape for 15-30 seconds, then cover it with a blank white or grey sheet and relax your gaze on to this for 15-30 seconds. Then look at the centre of the second (content) shape for 15-30 seconds, cover it as before and look at the blank sheet. Finally, look at the third – the combination – image for the same time, and finish as before, by looking at the blank sheet.

Do this with the eight sets, morning and evening. A complete session lasts about 20 minutes. Repeat for 2-3 weeks.

Alternatively, use only two sets at a time. Choose complementary sets, for example, Set 1 (red) followed by Set 5 (turquoise). Allow yourself the freedom to choose the colours of the sets intuitively.

Natural daylight or full-spectrum lighting (see p. 36) supplies the best light for the exercise.

| **Container** | **Content** | **Combination** |

Set 1

Set 2

Set 3

Set 4

The Platonic Solids

Tetrahedron
(4 x 3)
Associated with fire, man, sight,
recognition, consciousness, and the
colour red.

Octahedron
(8 x 3)
Associated with air, the bird, sound
(listening), pyramid healing energy,
and the colour yellow.

Icosahedron
(20 x 3)
Associated with water, the reptile,
taste, and the colour blue.

Hexahedron
(6 x 4)
Associated with earth, the mammal,
smell, and the colour green.

Dodecahedron
(12 x 5)
Associated with ether, spirit, touch,
and the colour violet.

Colour, shape, and Sacred Geometry

Ancient geometry begins with the One, the basic Unity, the representation of the wholeness of the universe. The Ancient Greeks (7th-2nd centuries BC) produced geometric shapes to try to articulate all the spaces and relationships, patterns, and proportions existing within the original sphere of creation. The shapes became known as the Sacred Geometry. Current Western scientific thinking now accepts the importance of patterns and proportional relationships between particles, and the notion that these (rather than the particles themselves) affect our perception.

Plato, a contemporary of the ancient geometricians, visualized the world as being composed of basic elements, each represented by a particular shape. Plato expressed them in five "Solids". The Platonic Solids are special versions of the Sacred Geometry. In each solid, the lengths of the sides are all equal, and all interior angles are equal. The elements are traditionally linked with colour – fire being seen as red, water as blue, and so on.

The Platonic Solids represent a blueprint for all the cell structures in the bodies of humans, animals, plants, and minerals. The two-dimensional coloured shapes used in healing are ultimately derived from the Platonic Solids.

The shapes based on triangles traditionally represent male energy; the hexahedron, built on the square, represents female energy. The dodecahedron, based on the pentagon, is the number of life (three male plus two female).

Working with coloured pigment

Printed or dyed colours present a useful way of treating with colour and maintaining progress between treatments with light. Some ailment treatments (see pp. 100, 102-3 and 107) are particularly suited to working with pigment colour. The general effects of using colour in interior decorating were discussed in Chapter One. The therapeutic use of these colours in clothes, silks, food, and the eye strengthening chart is described here.

When choosing colours, it is of course important to consider the appropriate shade. Try to find a tone that comes from the centre of the spectral colour, not too dark or too light.

Coloured clothes

The effects of wearing coloured clothes follow the general patterns already described (see p. 22). For example, wear blue to reduce high blood pressure; red to give you more energy and to increase low blood pressure. Experience has shown that wearing red can cure infertility that results from low body temperature combined with low blood pressure. Wear orange to combat depression; turquoise to enhance your immunity and to help inflammatory conditions.

In all cases, it is advisable to wear natural fibres because they allow the body to breathe. This refers not only to the exchange of air, but to the exchange of the finer colour energies in and out of the body.

Coloured silks

Silk is the finest material for the transmission of colour energies (see above). Allow yourself the luxury of using a large piece of silk to cover your undressed body, following the same colour guide as above. Lie down, ideally with full daylight on your silk-covered body, and listen to your favourite music for about 20 minutes. Do this three times each week for maximum effect.

Food

The different colours of food appeal to the eye. You should trust your intuition, and take in the colours of food that you choose naturally. If you follow your own guidance, and are not beguiled by outside influences such as advertising, you will be choosing food colours that your body needs.

The value of pigment in treatment

From the theory that describes solid objects as light energy that has slowed down (see p. 37), it follows that the pigment in a solid object is also a form of light energy reduced into matter. Pigment contains a memory of the energy of the light from which it arose. Plants contain this memory, which is why plant dyes are thought to be more effective in healing than artificial ones. Pigment cannot penetrate the body in the way that light does, so its healing properties are less powerful than those of light.

Pigment and light

The distinction between the effectiveness of pigment and light in healing is not absolutely clear. The pigment in clothes and silks, for example, is effective because of the light that penetrates through the coloured fabric and into the body.

The eye strengthening chart (see p. 106) produces a mixture of the effects of pigment and light. The eye fixes on the pigment colour and turns it back into light by way of the after image.

Eye strengthening chart

Eye problems represent a deterioration of the processes that produce vision. Too much work that entails focusing at the same distance over extended periods impairs the function of the eyes. The eye strengthening chart (see left) can be used to re-activate tired eyes, or to re-stimulate the eyes on a daily basis to maintain healthy vision. For more serious problems, use the eye healing lamp described on page 116.

Healthy tissue undergoes a continual transformation, taking new material in, and shedding useless cells. The eye strengthening chart gently moves the energies and the cell structures, re-introducing a more lively activity. The blue expands the blood vessels, and relaxes the organism, while the red increases the level of activity. This expansion-contraction stimulates the whole eye.

Healing with light

Light and its colours come from the original energies of creation. Light energy can penetrate all living substances; it affects the biochemical structures of plants, animals, and human beings (see p. 20).

There are many ways of introducing light into the body. The colour breathing and colour visualization exercises in Chapter Three can be as powerful as any other sort of treatment. But the lamps used for colour healing have a more direct influence. The colour energies penetrate your body and this does not depend on your ability to visualize.

Using the eye strengthening chart

Focus your eyes first on the blue octagonal shape. Maintain your gaze for 15-20 seconds. Then look at a blank sheet of white or grey paper for 15-20 seconds. The after image will appear, and then fade. Now look at the red shape, and repeat the exercise. Continue in this way, six times daily.

The colours reproduced in the chart below are not accurate for treatment purposes. You can obtain a printed copy (see Equipment, p. 124) and place it on a wall at eye level where you have access to it daily.

Container	**Content**	**Combination**

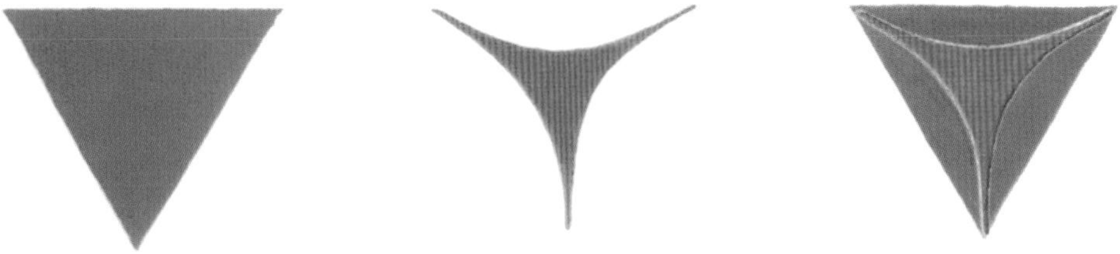

Set 5

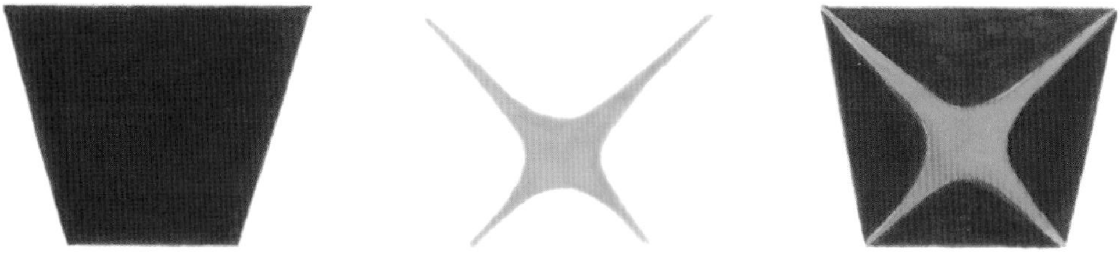

Set 6

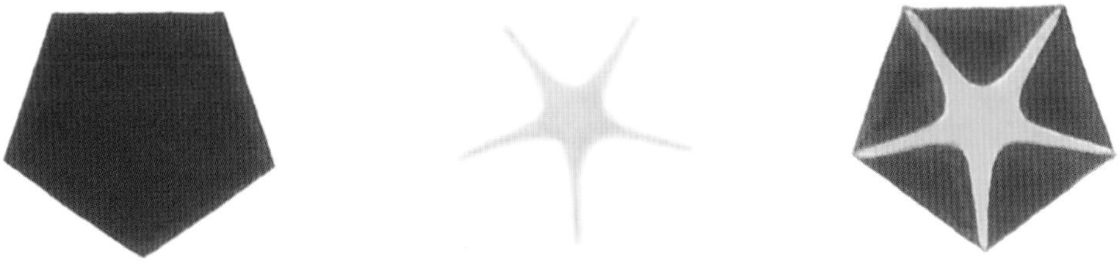

Set 7

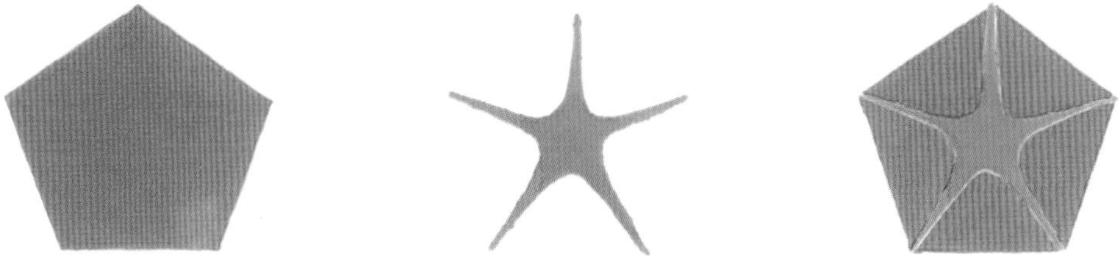

Set 8

This section (pp. 108-23) deals with the techniques of using the healing qualities of coloured light. It describes first the use of coloured lamps (pp. 108-13), one of the main healing sources in colour therapy. It then goes on to discuss other accessories available to practitioners, such as the eye healing lamp (p. 116) and the Hy-Co-Jet bath (p. 114). The final sections describe techniques you can use at home, such as solarized water (p. 115), and the use of oils (p. 117) and crystals (pp. 117-8).

Colour therapy instruments

Equipment for projecting coloured light on to a patient can be designed in various ways, but the first instrument to combine colour and form for this purpose was designed at Hygeia Studios in Gloucestershire, England, in 1969.

The colour therapy instrument uses a full-spectrum lamp housed in a box. One side of the box is designed to take a piece of frosted glass, a stained glass filter, and lastly a screen, or "mask", which controls the shape of the light aperture. In this way, the treatment colour can be combined with the particular shape that enhances its work (see p. 47). The shapes correspond to those already seen in the colour consciousness exercise (see pp. 102-3 and p. 107).

The high quality of the stained glass filter ensures that the full spectrum of the required colour is projected on to the patient. The filters are made by hand, but their chemical composition resembles the structure of the natural oxides found in jewels. Gold, silver, copper, magnesium, and cobalt are incorporated into liquid quartz, then mouth blown and cut into sheets.

Light treatment

Once the treatment colour has been determined, whether through spinal diagnosis, or aura analysis, or any of the other diagnostic techniques described in Chapter Five, the practitioner may decide to treat with coloured light using the colour therapy instrument.

Exposure to the treatment colour alternates with its complementary. The treatment colour orange alternates with blue; magenta with green; violet with yellow, and red with turquoise. The patient prepares for treatment by stepping into an all-white gown, so as not to distort the colours that penetrate through clothing to the body, and then sits or lies down in comfort about 6-8 feet (2m) from the colour therapy instrument. The two colours are set on a stand, the treatment colour above the complementary colour (see below).

In addition to combining colour and shape, the light treatment is delivered in a rhythmic way. The timing of these exposures is operated by a time control and is based on the proportions of the "golden mean" (see p. 38). The initial exposure to the treatment colour is ¾ minute, then the instrument switches to the complementary for 3¼ minutes. As the exposure to the treatment colour increases to 5¼ minutes, the length of the exposure to the complementary decreases to ¾ minute (see below). The total exposure time is 19¾ minutes, of which the treatment colour accounts for 12½ minutes, and the complementary 7¼ minutes, thus keeping to the "golden mean" proportions. An example of the times of exposure to a colour and its complementary is given below, shown in quarters of a minute.

The need for the complementary colour

Experience has shown that treatment with one colour only does not produce a healing result. It may improve the symptoms, which then revert to the pre-treatment condition on exposure to daylight. Research into treatment for high blood pressure has indicated that this is the case.

As all energy exists with its complementary energy, the use of the complementary colour in therapy makes a natural pattern for treatment.

Treatment times for coloured light

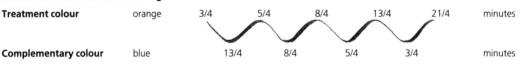

| Treatment colour | orange | 3/4 | 5/4 | 8/4 | 13/4 | 21/4 | minutes |
| Complementary colour | blue | 13/4 | 8/4 | 5/4 | 3/4 | | minutes |

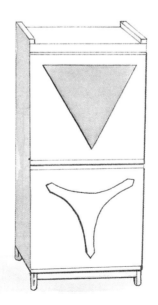

The colour therapy instrument
This instrument (left), *developed by the Hygeia Studios, provides full-spectrum colour defined in the shape that enhances that colour's effect* (see pp. 110–11). *The exposure to the treatment colour* (top) *and its complementary* (bottom) *is rhythmic and carefully timed* (see above).

The instrument is used in a darkened room to prevent daylight "diluting" the effects of the colours used in treatment.

At the end of each phase of colour, one light is dimmed gradually while at the same time the other is slowly turned up to full strength. The patient may have relaxed into sleep, which is a good sign, because this ensures that the colours are well absorbed.

After the treatment, or as the patient awakes, there might be an immediate emotional response, resulting from the release of blocked emotional energies. This can have an immediate effect on the colours of the aura. Grey discolourations, representing unaccepted energy may have been absorbed, and brown areas, the result of energy not being let go, may have lessened, or disappeared (see p. 89). The colours may generally have become brighter and clearer. Such changes may be "momentary" (24–72 hours), "temporary" (2–12 weeks), or permanent.

The treatment colours

MAGENTA
The key to magenta is the idea of *letting go*. Use it also where change is needed. Magenta induces spirituality – it brings with it a recognition of spiritual energies.

VIOLET
The keyword for using violet is *dignity*.

BLUE
The keyword for blue is *relaxation*.

TURQUOISE
The theme for the work of turquoise is *immunity*.

Mental
Use magenta if you need to let go of old thought patterns, or old memories.

Mental
Violet works on your feelings of self worth, your dignity, and your self respect. Use it if you tend to diminish yourself, and always feel that others can do better than you.

Mental
Use blue when you cannot think calmly, or when you have no patience with your thoughts; when you always feel determined you are hurrying.

Mental
Use turquoise when you are dominated by others; when you do not rely on your own thoughts, but throw them away and value other people's ideas more. In other words, use it when you lack immunity to other people's thoughts.

The safety of light treatments

Before starting colour therapy treatments it is wise to consult a trained practitioner. However, the treatments using coloured silk, clothes, and food can be used at home. If you select and use the wrong treatment colour, although you will not gain any benefit from the treatment, you will not do any lasting damage.

Treatments using coloured light are more powerful. It is important that the treatments given with the colour healing instruments described on pages 108–17 are only given by people trained in the use of the instrument. The correct timing of the light exposure is as critical as the selection of the correct colour for treatment. The wrong rhythm can create imbalances in the body's energy flow, and correcting these imbalances may require further treatment.

GREEN
The keyword for green is *balance*.

YELLOW
The central theme for yellow is *detachment*.

ORANGE
The keyword for orange is *joy*.

RED
The keyword for red is *energy*.

Mental
Use green if you tend to take your work home with you, in the metaphorical sense; equally, when you take your domestic matters into your work situation. Use it if you cannot keep your thoughts in balance; if they are dominated by one thing or another.

Mental
When you cannot detach yourself from other people's activity; you cannot make your own thoughts, or you become over-attached to an idea that you need to let go of, consider using yellow.

Mental
If you cannot enjoy your own mental processes, or just do not feel like using your brain to do anything, use orange.

Mental
If you lack mental energy even to think, and you do not want to get involved with anything, use red.

MAGENTA	VIOLET	BLUE	TURQUOISE

MAGENTA

Emotional
When old feelings no longer apply, magenta works on these unwanted emotions, allowing you freedom to let go of them and to grow and change.

VIOLET

Emotional
If you do not like your own feelings, or think they are of no interest, use violet. It is the colour most deeply associated with your feelings about who you really are.

BLUE

Emotional
If you cannot experience peaceful feelings, or feel ill at ease with your feelings, consider using blue.

TURQUOISE

Emotional
When you find you are laughing with other people, even when you do not under-stand what is funny, consider using turquoise. You may also find that other people's illnesses affect you; they make you feel ill, too.

Metabolic
For problems within the home; use magenta when you need to let go of old domestic patterns and make changes in the rhythm or conduct of the household, including meal times and any domestic routines.

Metabolic
Use violet if you lack respect for your home, or do not treat it in a dignified way. Violet is indicated when your home is just a place you use, rather than live in fully.

Metabolic
When you have no time for your home, your food, or your lifestyle, or if you are the type who snatches a quick sandwich in one hand and has a book in the other at the same time, you need blue treatment.

Metabolic
Turquoise works on the immunity of the cell. Use it when your health immunity is low, and you too readily catch infections.

Physical
This level affects the plan of the day or week. Use magenta if you need to set aside existing schedules and restructure the daily or weekly plan.

Physical
This refers to lack of self love, or lack of self appreciation. Use violet if you feel that you are not beautiful.

Physical
Try using blue when every-thing is rushed, when you never seem to have enough time for your daily tasks or your weekly schedule.

Physical
The habit of imitating others, or "keeping up with the neighbours", suggests the need for the colour turquoise. Use it when you cannot help being influenced by other people's style of living.

GREEN

Emotional
When you feel unbalanced by relationships that are no longer intact, treat with green.

Metabolic
Green induces balance in the household and in the body. Use it when your home or your health is unbalanced.

Physical
If your daily programme is unbalanced – you do not eat breakfast, or you skip lunch – or if you have the feeling that you cannot get things sorted out, think of using green in your healing.

YELLOW

Emotional
For people who cannot stand back from a situation; for a mother who rushes to her baby immediately at the merest sound, yellow is helpful.

Metabolic
This relates to the calcium uptake process in the body. Calcium accumulates at the joints through an inability to let it go. People over 40 years old may need yellow.

Physical
Use yellow to enable you to detach yourself from your material possessions – your old car, or curtains that you may have had for a long time and can no longer use, but feel unable to relinquish.

ORANGE

Emotional
Lack of joy or happiness in a relationship often goes unmentioned, but if you do not enjoy your emotional experiences you will need more of this colour. It is used to combat depression. If you overdo treatment with orange, the opposite feelings can set in: you become happy-go-lucky and irresponsible.

Metabolic
If your home circumstances do not give you joy, if you no longer enjoy meal times, or if you feel no joy when preparing food, treat with orange.

Physical
Treat unhappiness that permeates all your activities – a general lethargy, or a feeling that you can't be bothered with things – with orange. Endless procrastination suggests that you need orange.

RED

Emotional
You have not even enough energy to experience any emotions, or your emotions lack strength. You are too tired to bother with your emotions. All these symptoms suggest that you need red.

Metabolic
Use red if no energy is being put into the household; if everything is being done for convenience and not for the pleasure of doing it. If, for example, you are too tired to lay the table attractively before eating, or you rely on artificial room fresheners or any other prop to reduce the amount of effort needed in the house, try red.

Physical
Use red to counter physical apathy. It also raises blood pressure; it treats low blood pressure.

Coloured oils (right), *for massage or in baths, can be used to complement colour therapy treatments. Ideally the oils should be used freshly made (see p. 117).*

Colour healing accessories

You can use the range of colour healing accessories discussed in this section either in combination with the colour therapy instrument, or as healing tools in themselves. Refer to the chart on page 101 to see which ailments respond best to which treatment.

Hy-Co-Jet bath

By exposing yourself to coloured light in water, you can absorb the light frequencies over the whole surface of your body. The warmth of the water, combined with the massage from the jets at the sides of the bath, relaxes your muscles and makes your body more receptive to colour.

The Hy-Co-Jet bath may be fitted with any colour, but usually it is used with blue and its complementary, orange, to reduce stress, insomnia, and muscle tension. Fill the bath with water that is comfortably hot, and once you are in, switch on the jets alone for up to five minutes before starting the colour treatment. At this point, stop the jets, and enjoy the colours. The start button sets in motion a time control: the same timings apply as with the colour therapy instrument (see p. 109), so the coloured bath session ends after

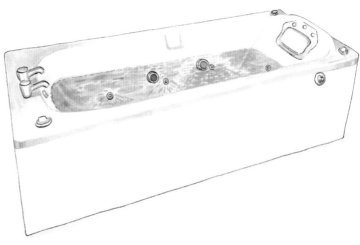

The Hy-Co-Jet bath
Jets of water from the sides of the bath relax the patient before the light treatment begins. An automatic time control mechanism controls the exposure to the treatment colour and its complementary.

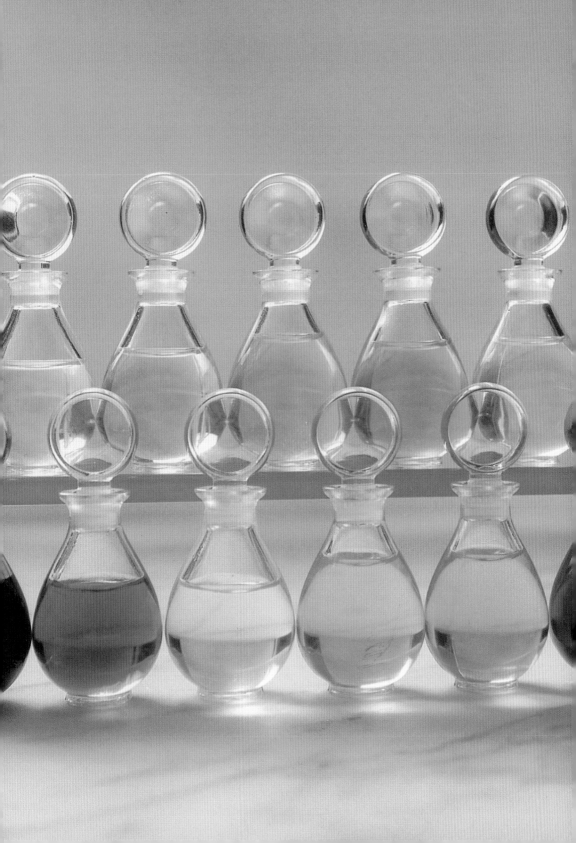

19¾ minutes. At this point the temperature of the water will have cooled slightly, to blood heat. Getting out at this point presents the least shock to the system. Play some soothing music during your bath to enhance the effects (see p. 118).

Water solarizer

The colours of light are thought to affect water at the molecular level, imbuing the water with the energies of the colour that it receives, as well as affecting its taste. Solarized water was used in Ayurvedic medicine in India from the 1st century AD, but it may have been first made there as long as 9000 years ago. It was also used for healing in Egypt about 4000 years ago.

To solarize water, surround a glass of still water with a full-spectrum filter of red or blue (see *Resources,* p. 124). Allow sunlight to shine through the glass for about two hours (longer on a cloudy day). Then drink the water slowly.

The taste changes according to the colour of the filter: red makes the water sour; blue sweetens it. Other colours produce a range of tastes between these two extremes. For this reason, only red and blue are usually used. Use the red filter as a stimulation – to help you wake up, for example. The blue solarized water has a relaxing effect, and is a good bedtime drink.

Eye healing lamp

Use the eye healing lamp for severe disturbances of the eye, such as cataracts, and glaucoma. It also improves short and long sight, by mobilizing the muscles of the iris, which control the shape of the lens.

The lamp has one colour aperture and two filters. Sit about three feet (0.7-0.9m) in front of the lamp, with the aperture at eye level. Move the turquoise and red filters over the aperture in turn, so that you see first the turquoise coloured light, then the red. Look at each colour for 20-30 seconds. Gaze at the white, black, or grey panel at the base of the lamp for 20-30 seconds between each colour; this allows the eye to produce the after-image colour (see p. 62), which relaxes the eye. Do this twice daily. Finish with the turquoise, and its after image, so that the eyes are completely relaxed at the end of the session. Consult your eye specialist to monitor the effects of the lamp.

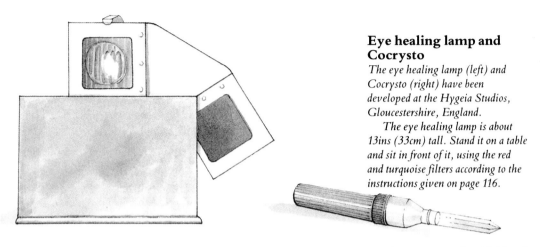

Eye healing lamp and Cocrysto
The eye healing lamp (left) and Cocrysto (right) have been developed at the Hygeia Studios, Gloucestershire, England.

The eye healing lamp is about 13ins (33cm) tall. Stand it on a table and sit in front of it, using the red and turquoise filters according to the instructions given on page 116.

The Cocrysto is a hand-held torch that uses the healing energies of crystals, programmed with the healing colour by a stained glass filter (see below) to bring colour energy into the chakras.

Oils

Coloured oils are made from pure oils by the addition of healing herbs and flowers and exposure to sunlight, often for days or weeks. This allows the oils to absorb the energy of the plants; the oil also changes colour, depending on which plant is used.

Use the oils to massage part or all of the body or in a bath. The particular energies of each oil may be soothing or energizing in their effects, depending on the plants used. Ideally, fresh oils should be used and always remember to follow the manufacturer's instructions.

Crystals

Crystals are concentrated forms of light energy that are produced in the absolute darkness of coal beds, clay beds, and other sedimentary rocks. Because of their structure, they can absorb instructions via the electronic messages from a computer. Using light and a coloured filter, a quartz crystal can be programmed for healing with that colour.

In the same way as the chakras are seen as being the energy centres of the human body, so the crystals are the energy centres of our planet Earth. By using crystals in healing, you will be able to tune your body to the healing energy of the planet.

In the same way as the chakras are seen as being the energy centres of the human body, so the crystals are the energy centres of our planet (see right). *By using crystals in healing, you can tune the body to the healing energy of the planet.*

Enhancing therapy with music

Music may be used as part of the treatment plan. It can be a powerful support to the work of colour treatment, in three ways.

First, background music can be used for its healing qualities. The composer JS Bach incorporated intervals into his music that bore the same relationship to each other as numbers in the Fibonacci series (see p. 38). These musical intervals create, in effect, the same "golden mean" proportions that are seen in classical architecture, and that are said to create a visual harmony. In the same way, music produces a vibratory harmony – healing sounds.

Second, musically qualified practitioners can develop personalized musical themes that stimulate the memory and the subconscious of the individual.

Third, the practitioner may encourage you to sing. This both helps you to express yourself freely, and to "retune" your body, by linking your mind, your body, and your emotions. The following three case studies indicate how a practitioner interprets patients' problems and demonstrates the way a course of colour therapy can progress.

Crystals are used in colour therapy to balance the chakra system of a patient (see p. 64). Clear and colourless quartz crystals are the most useful in colour healing. The colour crystal torch, or Cocrysto (see p. 117), focuses light through a stained glass filter and a clear quartz crystal to bring colour into the chakras. The patient should be dressed in white, as coloured clothing will distort the treatment colour. Hold the Cocrysto about one inch (2.5cm) from the patient's body, focusing the energies through visualization on to each chakra centre.

Combining treatments

Ideally all colour therapy should be supervised by a qualified practitioner. By getting to know the patient, the practitioner can use his or her professional judgement about how often to treat, and how many therapeutic methods to combine. It is quite usual to use two methods to maximize the effect. A practitioner will usually give a patient colour breathing exercises (see p. 54) or guided visualizations (see p. 52) that back up the work of the colour therapy instrument. Alternatively, the patient may receive advice on coloured clothing (see p. 105) to wear to maintain the effects. Treatments support each other best when identical colours are used.

Consult the chart on page 101 to see which ailments respond well to two or more methods used in combination. To a large extent, the choice of treatments is a practical solution to a particular problem. For example, it would be of little use to suggest a visualization to treat insomnia, as the images would be more likely to keep the patient awake than to induce sleep. Instead, if you are being treated for insomnia with the colour therapy instrument, you might choose to drink blue solarized water between treatments. You could also add colour breathing. If so, give yourself a break – ideally overnight – between drinking the solarized water and using the breathing techniques. This break allows your body to absorb the energy of the treatments.

Increasing the number of techniques or the exposure to colour does not necessarily speed the healing process. Too much colour cannot be absorbed by the body; you can "overdose" on colour just as you can on drugs. As a general rule, do not exceed one treatment in every 24 hours.

The following three case studies indicate how a practitioner interprets patients' problems and demonstrates the way a course of colour therapy can progress.

Case study – Trevor

Trevor's case was interesting because it showed very clearly that he was blocking some unhappy thoughts about his life. Following an operation for cancer, he was depressed and aimless. Aged 62, he was not looking forward to retirement.

He resented the fact that his wife worked long hours. Generally it was difficult to get him to talk about himself. Even when I asked about his hobbies, he said that his interest in woodwork had gone since he found it painful to get involved in an activity that was associated with the period before his illness.

Advice and treatment

The colour that came up from the spinal diagnosis was orange, specifically relating to the emotional area. One way to approach his problem of depression and his lack of ability to talk about himself was to get him involved in an activity that confronted his emotions. I encouraged him to take up woodwork again.

The colour yellow came up in the metabolic area at the next treatment. I asked him to work on a visualization to help him detach from painful memories of the past. I felt that the significance of his metabolic problem may be deep-seated, or too problematic to treat. Sometimes it can be more effective to tackle the problem via another avenue, as in the visualization. The operative factor was the colour, yellow, which gave the clue that detachment was needed.

After five treatments, Trevor's problems seemed to lift considerably, through working obliquely to encourage him to create change and acknowledge the areas of his life that he was blocking from his consciousness.

Case study – Natasha

Natasha came to me with a persistent problem of general weakness and tiredness. She felt unable to "get the day started". We talked about her life and I questioned her about her domestic life and her work. I wanted to know which of her activities she most enjoyed, and which of them she found unpleasant. After a long discussion it became clear that my client looked forward to nothing at all.

We talked about her eating habits, which are a key factor in the health of the metabolic activity in the body. "I usually eat anything that doesn't need to be prepared", she said. "Often I buy a sandwich or something that I can heat up quickly." Natasha lived alone, and had little opportunity for joining friends or family for lunch or dinner.

She was equally scathing about how she spent her spare time. Natasha wanted to write, but felt she had no chance of learning how to begin.

Advice and treatment

Natasha was obviously not getting enough nutrition from her food. This seemed to be more overriding than her frustrated ambition to write. Her spinal diagnosis showed the need for treatment with the colour green.

I treated her with this using the colour therapy instrument.

I continued the treatments over the next few weeks, following up problems with Natasha's digestion, by setting exercises for her to carry out at home. Turquoise showed up as the treatment colour at the second consultation. I gave her some turquoise paper, which she was to place over her abdomen, and use to enable her to practise colour breathing, taking turquoise in and breathing red out.

By incorporating fresh fruit and vegetables into her diet, and after the colour breathing, there were improvements in Natasha's digestion and in her energy level. She could now address her wish to write, and sounded much more clear about it. She continued colour breathing, taking turquoise in, and breathing red out.

When, at the next session, orange came up as a treatment colour, it was time to concentrate on her own fulfilment – to try writing, and to use this to bring more joy into her life. She seemed ready to begin. Before the next treatment, Natasha started writing. But she stopped her colour breathing, and this showed up in her reduced energy levels. Once Natasha understood that her own work was just as important as the therapy sessions, she started the exercises again. The successful outcome of the treatment was the publication of her first book a year later.

Case study – Melanie

I first met Melanie when she was nine years old. She did not speak or allow any eye contact. As soon as she saw me, she ran out of the house and raced around the garden on her bicycle.

Her father and mother told me that when she was two months old, Melanie had had an operation to remove a facial mark. After the operation, her mother noticed a change in Melanie, "It was as if I lost contact completely, I cannot describe it any other way." Her father enlarged on this, "The doctors admitted that it had been very difficult to bring Melanie round after the operation."

I realized that the shock of the operation had been too great for Melanie at that early age. The operation had shifted her protective aura away from her body (see pp. 88-9) and it had not returned to normal. The mental and emotional areas were not connecting with the metabolic and physical areas. Melanie seemed to hover above her body, unable to "connect" with it.

Both parents agreed that I should try to treat her. I knew that it would take many months, but they agreed to be patient.

Advice and treatment

For a whole year I treated Melanie, seeing her every three to four weeks. One day, her spinal diagnosis chart looked completely different from all previous ones. When I met Melanie again, she looked straight into my eyes.

Melanie continued to make eye contact during the next few months. By this time, I had made 26 spinal diagnosis charts. None of the active vertebrae in the emotional area of the early charts were paired, and there was no connection between the mental/emotional and the physical/metabolic areas. But by now, Melanie was producing more and more normal charts. After about three years of work, she began to speak. Her parents were delighted.

Today, when I meet Melanie, she seems very obviously a "normal" child. Anyone who met her without knowing her history would never suspect anything was wrong.

Melanie still dislikes reading, and, indeed, cannot, as yet, read fluently, nor does she like writing. But this is not surprising after such a history. A great deal of care and more patience has to be given to her. But in general, she is now a very happy, peaceful, and healthy young lady.

As the sun sets the colours of the evening do not fade into the colours of the night, but are still present at the deeper level of the invisible (right).

Finishing the healing process

Treatments with a practitioner might continue over a few weeks or a few months. A review of progress takes place at regular intervals. This gives both the patient and the practitioner the opportunity to reflect on the changes and to see how well the patient is responding to self treatment at home. Repeated colour diagnosis via the aura or using the spinal diagnosis, or the Colour Reflection Reading (see pp. 94-6), monitors these changes.

Before a patient stops treatment, the practitioner looks again at the patient's understanding of the connection between mind, body, and emotions (see p. 74). The key feature of healing is to accept the role of the emotions. If the emotional response, which is the first response, is not acknowledged, these stifled feelings begin to create problems in the mind and body. By encouraging the patient to feel involved with the emotions, not to be ashamed of them or frightened by them, the practitioner ensures that the patient enriches his or her life within. By acknowledging, too, the role of rhythm, at work, at home, and in eating habits, the patient will be taking care of the metabolic aspect of health. Rhythm is not the same as meaningless routine: it simply addresses the need for regularity, but also regular change. It is a way of acknowledging daily the role of complementary energies that keep us in health.

A patient who has received treatment from a colour therapist will not just feel better. Colour therapy introduces a new way of looking at colour, and because of this it can permanently enhance colour awareness. Colour becomes a new language for interpreting feelings, and recognizing the feelings of other people. It reconnects you to the rhythmic colour energies of the planet, and enhances the living qualities of all life forms. The subtle powers of colour that permeate you and all life will continually revitalize you.

BIBLIOGRAPHY

Abbott, A. *The Colour of Life* McGraw-Hill, New York,1947

Babbit, E. D. *The Principles of Light and Color*, Ed. Birren, The Citadel Press, Secausus New Jersey, USA,1980

Birren, F. *Color: A Survey in Words and Pictures*, University Books, New York,1956

—*The Symbolism of Color*, Carol Publishing, New York,1989

Critchlow, K. *Islamic Patterns* Thames and Hudson, London, 1976

Dewhurst-Maddock, O. *The Book of Sound Therapy*, Gaia Books Ltd, London,1993

Dreyfuss, H. *Symbol Source Book*, Van Nostrand Reinhold Company, New York,1984

Gimbel, T. *Form, Sound, Colour and Healing*, The CW Daniel Company Ltd, Saffron Waldon, UK,1987

— *Healing Through Colour*, The CW Daniel Company Ltd, Saffron Waldon, UK,1980

— *The Colour Therapy Workbook*, Element, UK,1993

Gregory, R. L. *Eye and Brain*, World University Library, London, 1966

Hunt, R. *The Seven Keys of Colour Healing*, The CW Daniel Company Ltd, Saffron Walden, UK,1968

Huntley, H. E. *The Divine Proportion*, Dover Publications Inc, New York,1970

Itten J. *The Art of Color*, Reinhold Publishing Corporation, New York,1961

— *The Elements of Color*, Van Nostrand Reinhold Company New York, 1970

Jackson, C. *Colour Me Beautiful*, Piatkus, London,1983

Liberman, J. *Light Medicine of the Future*, Bear & Company Publishing, Santa Fe, New Mexico,1991

Lüscher, M. *The Lüscher Color Test*, Pan Books,1970

Ott, J. *Health and Light*, Devin Edair Company, Old Greenwich Conn, USA

Shepherd, A. P. *A Scientist of the Invisible: An introduction to the life and work of Rudolph Steiner*, Hodder & Stoughton, London, 1954

Sun, H. & D. *Colour Your Life* Piatkus Books, London, 1992

Varley, H. *Colour*, Marshall Editions Ltd, London, 1980

Wills, P. *Colour Therapy*, Element, UK, 1993

Wills, P. & Gimbel, T. *16 Steps to Health and Energy*, Quantum (W Foulsham & Co Ltd), Slough, UK, 1992

Wood, B. *The Healing Power of Color*, Destiny Books, Vermont, 1984

RESOURCES
Associations, Institutes, and Societies

Anthroposophical Medical Association
Rudolph Steiner House
35 Park Road
London NW1 6XT

British Association for Counselling
1 Regent Place,
Rugby
Warwicks CV21 SPJ

The British Society of Dowsers
Sycamore Barn, Hastingleigh
Ashford, Kent TN25 5HW

The Institute of Complementary Medicine
PO Box 194, London SE16 Q7
SAE to *Registrar* for details of registration or practitioner referrals.

The International Association for Colour
46 Cottenham Road, Histon
Cambridge, CB4 9ES

Consultations, Courses, and Therapy

Colour Bonds Associates (Lilian Verner Bonds)
137 Hendon Lane
Finchley, London N3 3PR
Colour Relate Readings, Tape: The Healing Rainbow.

Hygeia Studios
The Hygeia College of Colour Therapy Ltd
Brook House, Avening,
Glos GL8 8NS

Environment consultancy service, counselling and therapeutic treatments; residential and non-residential courses in colour therapy and counselling

Living Colour
33 Lancaster Grove
London NW3 4EX
This organization was founded in 1984 by Howard and Dorothy Sun. It aims to bring more colour into people's lives by raising their awareness through a comprehensive range of courses, and counselling and therapy services:
Colour Reflection Reading; colour counselling; colour therapy; chakra balancing.
Colour Your Life introductory and foundation courses. Further courses in colour counselling, colour therapy, and colour analysis.
Colour consultancy services. Send SAE for general information or send £2 (£5 overseas) for full Programme Information Pack.

Universal Colour Healing
67 Farm Cresent
Wrexham Court
Slough, Bucks SL2 STQ

EQUIPMENT

Full Spectrum Lighting
Unit 1,
Riverside Business Centre
Victoria Street
High Wycombe
Bucks HP11 2LT
True-Lite Full Spectrum Fluorescent Lighting; SAD Portable Lightboxes

Hygeia Manufacturing Ltd
Hygeia Studios
Brook House, Avening
Glos GL8 8NS
Colour Space Illuminator; Pure Light Lamp; Crystal Lamp; Eye Healing Lamp; Hygeia Colour Wall; Hygeia Colour Therapy Instrument; Coloured Silks; Stained Glass; Eye Strengthening Chart

Pool Services Ltd
Unit 12-14 Woodside Park
Industrial Estate
Catteshall Lane
Godalming, Surrey GU7 ILG
Hy-Co-Jet Hydro Colour Therapy Jet Bath

AUTHOR'S ACKNOWLEDGEMENTS

I would like to extend my very special thanks to my wife Honor, who has offered objective opinions on the writing of this book. My thanks go also to Pauline Wills, who gave practical advice on my writing and to Eleanor Lines at Gaia, who advised me on the content of the book. My staff, Doreen Cox and Rita Legg, have been very supportive, despite my occasional bouts of disgruntledness. Lastly, I should like to acknowledge the inspiration I have received from Father Dr Andrew Glazewski and Sir George Trevelyan who have given me insight into the spiritual meaning of healing; and Rudolf Steiner while I grew up in Dornach (1924–1939).

PUBLISHER'S ACKNOWLEDGEMENTS

Gaia Books Ltd would like to thank Rachel Adams, Suzy Boston, Ursula Browning, Gill Cormode, Fritz Fuchs, Natasha Goddard, Stuart Hall, Pamela Jenkins, Kate McNulty, Philip Parker, Kitty Parker-Jervis, Lesley Parry, Katherine Pate, Sonya Richards, Robert Rose, Howard Son, Susan Walby, and Nan Wise for editorial and production work; Mary Warren for editorial assistance and the index; Select Typesetters; Global Colour, Malaysia.

PHOTOGRAPHIC CREDITS

pp, 2-3,11, 14, 23, 42, 51, 55, 58, 78, 87, 98, 123, **Comstock;** p 6 Manfred Cage/**Science Photo Library**; p. 19 **Sonia Halliday Photographs**; p. 27 Hugh Palmer/**IPC Magazines Ltd.1989, Robert Harding Syndication**; p. 30 David Parker/**Science Photo Library**; p 35 Fred Burrell/**Science Photo Library**; p.38 **Paul Brierley Photos**; p.75 Lynne Brotchie/**The Garden Picture Library** p.115 Philip Dowell/**Gaia Books** p.119 Roberto du Gugliemo/**Science Photo Library.**

index

Bold type indicates main entry

after-images 40, 105, 106, 116
ageing process 20-1, 50, 76
AIDS 101
ailments 41, 101 *see also*
    disease; illness
analysis of spine 70-3, 93
Ancient Egyptians, Greeks
    and Romans 21, 116
Angelico, Guido di Pietro 60
angina pectoris 101
animals 61
Aristotle 33
art therapy 81, 96-7
arthritis 101
artificial dyes 24, 105 *see*
    also pigments
artificial light 20, 37
associations *see under* colour
asthma 101
astral body 62-3
auras 61, **62-8,** 80, 90
    changes, 76, 84, 86, 88-9
    discolouration 86-9
    energies 67, 76
    perception 66-7
    structure 62-5
awareness *see under* colour
Ayurvedic medicine 116

Bach, Johann Sebastian 118
balance of energies 74
base chakra 88
baths and bathing 114-16
Bauhaus School 22-3
bedrooms 25
black 23, 97
blocked energies 23, 85, 86,
    88, 111
blood pressure 101, 113
blue 20, 23, 54
    in auras 64, 88
    in decoration 25-6, 29
    form and senses 47-50
    and personality 94-7
    spinal diagnosis 72, 93
    in treatments 100-13
Botticelli, Alessandro 60

brain 10, 20, 33, 46, 48, 102
    altered states 67-8
brainwaves 60, 67-8
breathing 50, 52, 89, 101
    technique 54
brown 88, 89, 97, 111

cancer 101
case studies 85, 120-1
cataracts 116
causal body 62-3
chakras 64-5, 74, 76
    energy 67, **86-8,** 89, 90
Chartres Cathedral 18-19
charts
    aura discolouration 88
    chakra functions 64
    colour consciousness
        exercise 103
    colour and form 47
    colour and senses 48
    decoration summary 28-9
    dowsing the spine 71-3
    eye strengthening 106-7
    light treatment times 109
    personality assessment 94-5
    Platonic solids 104
    spinal diagnosis 91-3
    treatment colours 110-13
    treatment techniques 101
childhood 45, 76, 86
children 16, 20, 24, 82, 86
Chinese teachings 21, 68
choleric temperament 77
circulation of energy 82-3
Cleveland Hospital (England) 76
clothes 21-2, 101, 105, 108, 111
Cocrysto (torch) 117, 118
coding *see under* colour
colds 101
colour
    associations 16-17, 45, 46,
        48, 50, 84
    awareness 45, 48-9, 122
    coding 16-17, 26, 45
    commercial use 26
    effects 18, 20, **42-57**
    energies **66-77,** 80, 81
    history and science, 21, 33
    meanings 97
    spectrum 33-4
colour blindness 32-3
Colour Reflection Reading 81,

    94-6, 122
complementarity 40-1
complementary colours 39, 62
    in diagnosis 72-3, 91-3
    in treatment 109
consciousness 68, 81
cosmetics 22, 23
cosmic energy 36, 37, 83
counselling 84, 85, 96
crown chakra 88
crystals 21, 117-19
cyan 38, 39
cycles of illness 81

darkness 16, 37, 56
decor *see* interior decoration
depression 101, 113
design and pattern 76
diagnosis 13, 21, 80-5
    aura perception **86-9**
    spinal analysis **90-3**
dicyanin 66
diet 86 *see also* foods
digestive disorders 101
discolouration of aura 86-9
disease 80, 82 *see also*
    ailments; illness
dowsing 60, 66, 69-70, 80-1
    spinal analysis 71-3, 90
drugs 82, 89, 90
Druids 48

eczema 101
effects of colours 18, **42-57**
ego 62-3
eight-colour spectrum 40
Einstein, Albert 33
electro-convulsive therapy 89
electromagnetic energies 10, 33, 44
    spectrum 34-8
elements (five) 48, 104
emotions 12, 86-8, 92-3, 112-13
    and colour 25, 45-6
    energies 72-3, 74
    in healing 101, 122
energies 66, 72-3, 77
    balance and imbalance 21,
        70, 74, 85
    blocks 85, 86, 88
    chakra 67, 86-8, 89, 90
    circulation 74, 82-3, 111
    cosmic 36, 37, 83

electromagnetic 10, 33-8, 44
  input and output 60-1, 82-3
  light 18, 20, 106
  spectrum 18, 20, 34-5
enhanced colour response 49, 118
etheric sheath 62-3, 65, 89
eurythmy 56-7
evolution, aura 61
exercises 67
  colour breathing 54
  colour consciousness 100, 102-3
  meditation 52
  personality assessment 94
  relaxation 52
  visualization 52
exhaustion 90
eyes and eyesight 20, 32, 102
  healing lamp 116-17
  strengthening 101, 106-7

Fibonacci series 37, 38, 109, 118
Fibonacci, Leonardo 38
finger dowsing 70
five elements 104
fluorescent lighting 28
foods 86, 101, 105
form 37, 46-7
formation of matter 61
Four Humours doctrine 21
frequency 36
full-spectrum lamps and
  light 21, 23, 36-7

gemstones 21, 48
geometry: Sacred 104
glaucoma 116
Goethe, J W von 33
golden mean 38, 109, 118
green 23, 54, 57
  in auras 64, 88
  in decoration 25-6, 28
  form and senses 47-8
  and personality 94-7
  spinal diagnosis 73, 93
  in treatments 104-13
grey 23, 88, 89, 97, 111

haloes and wings 60
harmonic intervals 38
harmony 22-3, 118
healing 22, 102, 105-13, 122

charts 110-13
  instruments 108-17
health 72-3, 76, 81-3
hearing 48
heart chakra 88
Hippocrates 76-7
history, colour 21, 33
hobbies 84
home decor 24-5
hospitals 24, 25
Hy-Co-Jet bath 108, 114
Hygeia Studios 108, 109, 117
hypothalamus 20

illness
  diagnosis **80-3,** 88-9, 97
  treatments 101-13
imaging 60
imbalances of energy 21, 70, 84, 85
indigo 56
inflammation 101
infrared 18, 36
inner harmony 23
insomnia 101, 102, 114, 118
instruments, healing 108-17
interactions
  of energy 60
  of opposites 41
interior decoration 16, 24-8
  colour summary chart 28-9
intuition 45-6
Itten colour wheel 22
Itten, Johannes 22-3

Kilner screen 66
Kilner, Walter John 66
Kirlian photography 66
kitchens, decor 25

lamps 21, 116-17
lethargy 101, 113
light
  artificial 20, 28, 36
  and the body 32-3, 37
  energy 18, 20, 106
  full-spectrum 36-7
  physiology 32
  and pigment 38-9
  and plant growth 20, 60
  visible 18, 36
light treatments **106-11**

safety 111
lighting 28, 36-7
lunar effects 60
Lüscher colour test 81, 97
Lüscher, Dr Max 26, 97

magenta 47, 54
  in auras 64, 88
  in decoration 25, 29
  and personality 94-5
  spinal diagnosis 73, 93
  in treatments 108-13
make-up see cosmetics
massage 21, 49
matter formation 61
meaning of colours 97
meditation 18, 52, 60, 68
melancholic temperament 77
memory loss 101
mental activity 92-3, 110-11
metabolic body 62-3
  function 72-4, 92-3, 112-13
migraine 101
  case study 85
mineals 61
moon see lunar effects
movement 56-7, 81
music: therapeutic use 118

negativity 50, 80, 82, 88, 90
Nei Ching 21
Newton, Isaac 33

obsessions 101
oils: coloured 21, 117
opposites 40-1
orange 47, 54
  in auras 64, 88
  in decoration 25-6, 29
  and personality 94-6
  spinal diagnosis 73, 93
  in treatments 110-13
"overdosing" with colour 118

packaging 26
pain 82
patterns 66, 76
pendulum dowsing 13, 69-70
perception, aura 66-7
personal encounters 100-1

personality assessments 81, 94-5
phlegmatic temperament 77
photography 17, 66
photosynthesis 60
physical function 72-4, 92-3, 112-13
physiology 18, 20, 32
pigments 22, 24, 38-9, 105
pineal (crown) chakra 20, 88
pituitary (brow) chakra 20, 66, 88
Planck, Max 33
plants 61, 105
  growth 20, 38, 60
Plato 33, 104
Platonic solids 46, 104
practitioners 80, 84, 94,
  100-2, 111
precious stones *see*
  crystals, gemstones
primary colours 22, 38-40
prisms 34-5
psychological tests 81
psychology of colour 45-6
puberty 76, 82
Pythagoras 33

quartz 117, 118

radio waves 36, 37
rainbows 18, 33
red 20, 23, 50, 57
  in auras 64, 88
  breathing 50, 54
  in decoration 26, 28
  form and senses 47-8
  and personality 94-7
  spinal diagnosis 73, 93
  in treatments 102-13
relaxation 29, 50, 52
rheumatism 101
rhythms 73, 77, 122

sacral chakra 74, 88
Sacred Geometry 104
safety: in light therapy 111
sanguine temperament 77
Sanskrit 64
schools 24
science of colour 32-40
Seasonal Affective Disorder
  (SAD) 21, 37
seasonal light 17, 20, 37

secondary colours 22, 38-9
self-awareness 82
sensations, bodily 90
senses 16, 46-9 *see also*
  sight
sexuality 64, 74-6
shape *see* aura changes; form
shapes, coloured 94-5, 102-3,
  110-15
shock 68, 88-9
sight 32-3, 48, 49, 101
    see also eyes
    treatments 116-17
silicon 117
silks 21, 101, 105, 111
singing: as therapy 118
skin 23, 32
sleep 61 *see also* insomnia
smell (sense) 48
solar plexus chakra 88
solarized water 21, 49, 101, 116
solids 61
sound 37, 48
spectrum
  colour 33-4
  electromagnetic 18, 20, 34-5, 37-8
Spinal Diagnosis Chart 74, 90-3
spine and spinal analysis 72-3, 80
  diagnosis 90-3
  dowsing 69-71, 90
spirituality 71, 102
stained glass 18, 117
Steiner, Rudolf 25, 56, 76
stroke therapy 100, 102
subconscious 81
Sun, Dorothy and Howard 94
sunlight 18, 36-7, 60

talking about colour 50
taste 48, 49
temperaments 76-7
tension 50
tertiary colours 22
throat (thyroid) chakra 88
thymus chakra 88
Tibetan teachings 64
touch 48, 49
toxins 89
treatments 88-9, 91, 112
  charts 101, 112-13
  combined therapies 118, 120-1
  use of colour 109, 112-13
  use of light 106-11

use of music 118
tungsten lighting 28
turquoise 47
  in auras 64, 88
  in decoration 25, 28
  and personality 94-5
  spinal diagnosis 72, 93
  in treatments 102-3, **106-13**

ultraviolet 18, 20, 36

variations, aura 76-7
vertebrae 69, 70, 72-3, 90
violet
  in auras 64, 88
  in decoration 25, 29
  form and senses 47-9
  and personality 94-5, 97
  spinal diagnosis 72, 93
  in treatments 104, 110-12
visualization 50, 52, 54, 89, 118
visually impaired 12, 32-3, 49

Waldorf School, Gottingen 24
water 49
  solarized 116
  in therapy 114
wave energy 33
wavelength 36
white 23, 26, 29
wholeness 40
wings and haloes 60
witnesses (dowsing) 70
workplaces 24-6

yellow 23, 54, 57
  in auras 64, 88
  in decoration 25-6, 28
  form and sense 47-8
  and personality 94-5
  spinal diagnosis 73, 93
  in treatments 104-13

zodiac signs 48